NIRAD C. CHAUDHURI

Many Shades, Many Frames

Oxford, 1991.

NIRAD C. CHAUDHURI

Many Shades, Many Frames

Dhruva N. Chaudhuri

Foreword: Khushwant Singh

NIYOGI
BOOKS

Published by

NIYOGI
BOOKS

D-78, Okhla Industrial Area, Phase-I
New Delhi-110 020, India

Tel: 91-11-26816301, 49327000
Fax: 91-11-26810483, 26813830

email: niyogibooks@gmail.com
www.niyogibooks.com

Design: Write Media

ISBN: 978-81-89738-90-7

Year of Publication: 2011

Printed at: Niyogi Offset Pvt. Ltd., New Delhi, India

To the memory of all
creative geniuses from
Bengal who went out to
the world with their art
and did India proud

The University of Oxford awarded Nirad C. Chaudhuri an Honorary Degree of Doctor of Letters at its Encaenia ceremony, March 1990.

Contents

Displaying the Commander of the British Empire (CBE) medal, which Nirad Chaudhuri received in 1992.

Foreword

The Immortal Nirad

Nirad Chaudhuri was the most outstanding intellectual I had the privilege of befriending. His encyclopaedic knowledge about everything that mattered has become legendary. If you wanted to know anything about history, literature (any country), science, natural phenomena, art, culture, etc, without having to wade through tons of reference books, all you had to do was to ask Nirad Babu to get the right answers. I have yet to meet another person with as much information stored up in his brain. Despite that, I have never heard him brag or indulge in self-praise.

Another unique feature of Nirad's was his style of writing. It was flawless and grammar-perfect. Everything he wrote was a sample of lucid prose, evocative and challenging. Many critics questioned his assumptions but none could fault him on his basic theses or his relentless logic.

Nirad Babu was an extremely conservative man, dedicated to his wife, regarded marriage as a sacrament and observed Victorian decorum in the society of women. Once, when returning home from one of my parties, he looked around for his wife and asked, 'Where is that big boiler, which keeps this little engine going?' Another time when I was going abroad he came to see me to get formal permission to call on my wife when I was away.

He was also a man of rectitude. Although he was on straitened circumstances most of his life, twice when I tried to put money in his way he turned down my proposals. One was from the Government of India to work on a booklet on the plight of East Pakistanis fleeing to India in large numbers; the other a generous offer from Mr Birla to give him any amount of money in any currency for the rest of his life. Nirad Babu rejected the Government's proposal with contempt and Birla's offer with a polite note saying 'no thank you'.

An enigma about Nirad Babu was his unadulterated adoration of the English and the British Raj. When he went to his office at the All India Radio he dressed himself like an Englishman with *sola topi*, neck tie and a suit. When going out to dinner, he wore a top hat, black bow, coat and trousers. At home he wore a *dhoti* and sat on the floor to read or write.

Nirad had a quick temper. Whenever he felt he had been slighted, he exploded like a volcano: 'You cur! Apologise or I will give you a shoe-beating.' Once he actually hammered a colleague with a glass paperweight and drew blood. He never lost his temper with me and never went beyond calling me a fool.

I cherish his memory and I am glad that his son Dhruva, who knew him better than anyone, has put the memories of his distinguished father in a book. I hope it will be widely read by Nirad Babu's innumerable admirers.

Khushwant Singh

Preface

My Earnest Plea and Word of Thanks

I hope all my readers will understand that it was more than a difficult task for me to write the text of this illustrated biography of my father, once The Unknown Indian. Nirad C. Chaudhuri had reached the pinnacle of his fame by writing no less than three of his own biographies in English as well as two in Bengali. In addition, my mother Amiya Chaudhurani, then well into her eighties in age, published the first two volumes of her own biographies where she described her married life and other interesting details about my father. While all these seven books written by my parents proved to be invaluable as I attempted to present Nirad Chaudhuri's life once again to my readers, I thought of making the photographs, mostly taken by me, as well as reproductions of a few rare documents, as important as the written text. I hope this view will be acceptable to all including many of my father's admirers.

Now, having made my objective of doing this biography somewhat clear, I would like to thank my late parents from whom I drew all the inspiration to complete this book. I express my heartfelt thanks to the famous author, and almost a mentor to me, Sardar Khushwant Singh. After hearing that I was keen to have the foreword of this book written by him, I was asked to visit him for a drink at one of

Surrounded by books: Nirad Chaudhuri in his library with his German Shepherd, Poppy.

his famous evening gatherings at Sujan Singh Park. After I had had my choice of Scotch, he surprised all those assembled there with the foreword, 'The Immortal Nirad', written in his own hand. I was truly overwhelmed, and now I apologise with folded hands for the long delay in completing this book.

Dipendranath Mitra, a stalwart in the world of publishing in India, and a family friend of many years, read the manuscript with the eye of a veteran publisher. He came to my rescue at a critical stage of writing the text and I can hardly find words adequate enough to thank him for his kind efforts. And then, almost at the last stage, my daughter Satarupa agreed to go through the entire copy with the eyes of a well experienced editor that she is. I am really grateful to her for the effort and time she spared in spite of her busy schedule and responsibilities as an Editorial Manager at Oxford University Press, India. My cousin, Professor Krishna Bose, former Member of Parliament and now the Chairperson of the Netaji Research Bureau, Kolkata, not only gave me all the help while writing the biography of her Mejo Kaka (middle uncle) but also provided a rare and only photograph of my father typing *The Autobiography of An Unknown Indian* dated August 1947. I am really grateful to her for this kind help.

I am grateful to Bikash D Niyogi, Managing Director of Niyogi Books, along with his co-publisher and wife Tultul Niyogi for their efforts in not only publishing this book but also keeping me on track in order to complete this biography. I am also grateful to the editors and designers of Write Media who spared no efforts to give the final shape to this book and to cooperate with all my requests and demands.

For the dispatches and photographs I would like to thank Shrabani Basu, author and special correspondent of the Ananda Bazaar group of newspapers in London. Also, a special thanks to journalist and friend, Amit Roy, based in London, for sending many interesting comments on Nirad Chaudhuri to *The Telegraph* of Kolkata.

For allowing me to photograph or use the available photographs I have to thank the following organisations and individuals: Netaji Research Bureau, Kolkata; Netaji Subhas Bose Open University, Kolkata and Himanish Goswamy for the two photographs taken by the late Parimal Goswamy in the thirties. Moira Pavelin from Oxford was kind enough to photograph the unveiling ceremony of the Blue Plaque at Lathbury Road, Oxford, and Satarupa Chaudhuri.

Of course, there may be, and will be, many others who should have been mentioned but I hope they will be generous enough to forgive me for the lapse of memory.

A Typical Welcome

Nirad Chaudhuri checking a proof copy of his book, Three Horsemen of the New Apocalypse, *Oxford, 1997.*

It was a late summer evening in 1997 when I opened the creaking garden gate of 20 Lathbury Road, Oxford. At some distance a clock on the belfry of St Anthony's College on Woodstock Road struck nine. While the Victorian semi-detached house stood silent and towering at the end of the front garden, only a single bay window on the ground floor had a warm glow of light that indicated that Father, the 'Unknown Indian', was not only awake but was perhaps working. For someone who was at the threshold of completing a century in his life this was indeed remarkable.

As I walked up to the front door, trailing my suitcase, the air around Father's garden was redolent with the overwhelming fragrance of a flowering plant called camellia. This particular bush had been planted many years ago. Father had to struggle hard for its survival under a spreading horse-chestnut tree, which was a favourite of Charles Parr who lived on the top floor of the house. Ever since my parents had moved into this house in 1982, the two old men, Charles Parr and Nirad Chaudhuri, were often at loggerheads over the choice of planting certain trees and shrubs.

For fifteen long years every visitor, or even strangers, would admire this particular garden, hailing it as the most beautiful one on Lathbury Road. However, at times they were rather surprised to see a tiny old man dressed in a *dhoti* and a thick woollen pullover, working single-handedly in a garden blazing with a variety of flowers ranging from tulips and rhododendrons to crimson-red climbing roses. But that summer evening when I arrived, this garden had an indifferent and neglected look, which though not apparent before perhaps reflected the increasing physical shortcomings that Father had begun to face. Feeling somewhat saddened, I opened the front door with a

Standing outside his residence, 20 Lathbury Road, Oxford, 1994.

spare latchkey, which after Mother died in the early autumn of 1994 was always with me whenever I travelled from New Delhi to Oxford.

After entering the hallway, which was overlooked by a golden mask of the ancient Egyptian king Tutankhamun, I saw that the solid oak wood door of the drawing room was wide open. Looking inside, I saw Father sitting in a corner of the room, poring over a small book. The sombre appearance of that half-darkened room with Father reading with great concentration was so overwhelming that I could not help but remain quiet for a minute or two.

Nirad Chandra Chaudhuri, always a frail man and now somewhat shrivelled because of age, sat on a Regency armchair once used by his wife. In the glow of a single lamp placed above his shoulder, Father was correcting a proof copy of his latest book, *Three Horsemen of the New Apocalypse*. From the inside, through the large bay window, whose curtains were not yet drawn, I could see clusters of the white camellia flowers against the deep blue of the twilight sky along with a few gables of the houses, which are typical of North Oxford.

Dressed, as usual, in a combination of a thick woollen pullover and a *dhoti*, Father took a good part of a minute after hearing me greet him to look up from the immediate task of correcting his book. 'Why are you so late this time?' was his blunt question, which revealed a characteristic obsession about punctuality. My explanation that I had to act as a gallant knight to a young lady from Assam who was travelling alone to meet her

In the hallway of his house under a mask of the Egyptian king Tutankhamun, 1993.

husband studying at Oxford did not seem to cut much ice. Instead, Father pointed towards a new reproduction of a painting of a lake by Monet, hung over the mantelpiece. He seemed to become totally absorbed in describing its beauty and his various associations with that painting including those with certain lakes that he had visited in the USA, Canada and Israel. For many years, that very place above the mantlepiece had been reserved for an original Daniel lithograph depicting the Dashaswamedh Ghat of Benares (now Varanasi). At that moment, I couldn't but help recollect how this urge for acquiring expensive art objects, rare books or even vintage wine had created difficulties for my mother and me, more than once over the years.

Somewhat disappointed with my less than warm admiration for the new acquisition, he waved me off towards the dining room and the kitchen. Peering into the refrigerator as well as glancing at the shelves of the larder, I was met yet again with Father's extravagant and flamboyant tastes. All that I could find there were two jars of Russian caviar, a full pot of salted seafood called 'Gentleman's Relish' and a large portion of smoked salmon from Canada wrapped in a packet of golden foil. Apart from these delicacies, there was

Working in his garden, considered one of the most beautiful on Lathbury Road, 1993.

a ceramic jar of bitter English marmalade from Fortnum & Mason. For someone as famished as me, there was not a single slice of bread, or any eggs, which could be made into an impromptu meal. I had to satisfy my hunger with some hard soup sticks, washed down with a glass of cold milk. Later, some chocolate bars, bought on an impulse from the duty-free shop at Dubai airport, served as a dessert. As I was about to finish that apology of a meal, Father walked in with a triumphant look on his face and announced that he had just finished correcting his latest book.

I was desperate for some sleep after the long flight and a tiresome stopover at Dubai, but Father wanted me to listen to a new recording of Beethoven's second symphony on his exclusive high-fidelity sound equipment. While listening to the lovely refrain from the slow movement of that symphony, I was reminded of the warm and romantic association that this particular piece of music had with Father's life. He often listened to this symphony on a borrowed gramophone with Mother in their early years. This association of Beethoven's music also reminded me of a story about the first wedding night of my parents. Left to themselves in the bridal chamber, Father went on to quiz his new bride regarding Beethoven and the correct spelling of his name. To his total surprise and certain discomfiture, Mother slowly but correctly spelt B E E T H O V E N.

Nirad Chaudhuri at his prolific best, writing under the warm glow of a green lamp, 1997.

I was in bed for only a few hours when dawn came; sunshine streamed in through the large French windows of the room where I was sleeping. Familiar with Father's early morning habits, I tiptoed out into the entrance hall and saw that a lamp in the drawing room had already been switched on. Nirad Chaudhuri was sitting hunched on the carpet and was deeply absorbed in writing. His favourite table lamp with a green glass shade was positioned just a couple of inches away from his head. The thick felt pen he now used for writing on the ruled sheets of paper meant that he was writing in Bengali, probably an article for the festival number of a leading Bengali magazine called *Desh*. Seeing me enter the room, he asked for a cup of coffee to be made as quickly as possible. While the water was being heated, I could not resist the temptation of using my camera to capture that scene of a writer, about to touch a hundred years and yet writing with a concentration that would be considered amazing. Later, after taking a sip or two of that highly sugared coffee laced with condensed milk, he read to me a deeply moving account of his views on life and the inevitability of death.

Early Days

An East Bengal village; a 1911 photograph taken by Nirad Chaudhuri's uncle.

Soon after the antique clock on the mantlepiece of the drawing room chimed seven, Father jumped up from the carpet on which he was writing and, with agility not usual at his age, drew the heavy curtains of the bay window aside. The prospect of a clear and bright day seemed to cheer him considerably. After finishing a breakfast of cereal and milk—the only items available in the house—Nirad Chaudhuri was ready to talk about his young days in Kishorganj, his ancestral village Banagram and his mother's village called Kalikutch, all in East Bengal, now Bangladesh.

He began by mentioning the oft-repeated fact that he was born in Kishorganj on 23 November 1897, or 9 Augrhyan 1304, according to the conventional Bengali almanac. His father Upendra Narayan Chaudhuri had moved from Banagram to Kishorganj, a small sub-divisional town, to

earn a livelihood as a *mukhtar* at the local court. *Mukhtars* were lawyers of a rank lower than advocates but could argue cases that were only criminal in nature.

One of the main reasons for my grandfather leaving his ancestral home, as well as the easy life of a *zamindar*, or a landlord, was because of his family running into difficult times owing to the extravagance of his ancestors. However, his mother, a person with a strong character, made sure that her only son attended high school first and later studied law in the district town of Mymensingh. Almost as in a fairy tale, all expenses for Grandfather's education were met with gold coins or *mohrs* found in a metal pot by this lady when digging for some arum roots to cook the midday meal. These *mohrs* had been minted from the era of Mughal Emperor Jahangir and long after my great-grandmother died, some of those *mohrs* would help my grandfather tide over financial difficulties, whenever required, down to his last days in the holy city of Benares, where he died of a sudden cerebral stroke at the age of sixty-seven.

The other reason why my grandfather wanted to move to Kishorganj was because of my grandmother Sushila Devi's continuing unhappiness in Banagram. After the death of her first infant son she felt she could no longer remain in a joint family and she persuaded Grandfather to set up a separate household in Kishorganj as well as earn an independent living as a lawyer. Later, she often recounted to her children that when their father had earned eight *annas* or half-a-rupee as his legal fees, she would cook a sumptuous meal of *luchis* or *puris*, fried in real ghee, along with mutton curry, a rare treat in Banagram.

Father then went on to describe Kishorganj. According to him, there were no more than six or seven brick houses in the entire town. All houses, including my grandfather's, were

Facing page: Sprawled on the carpet...this is how Nirad Chaudhuri wrote his articles in Bengali.

A river landscape of Bangladesh with the Garo Hills in the background.

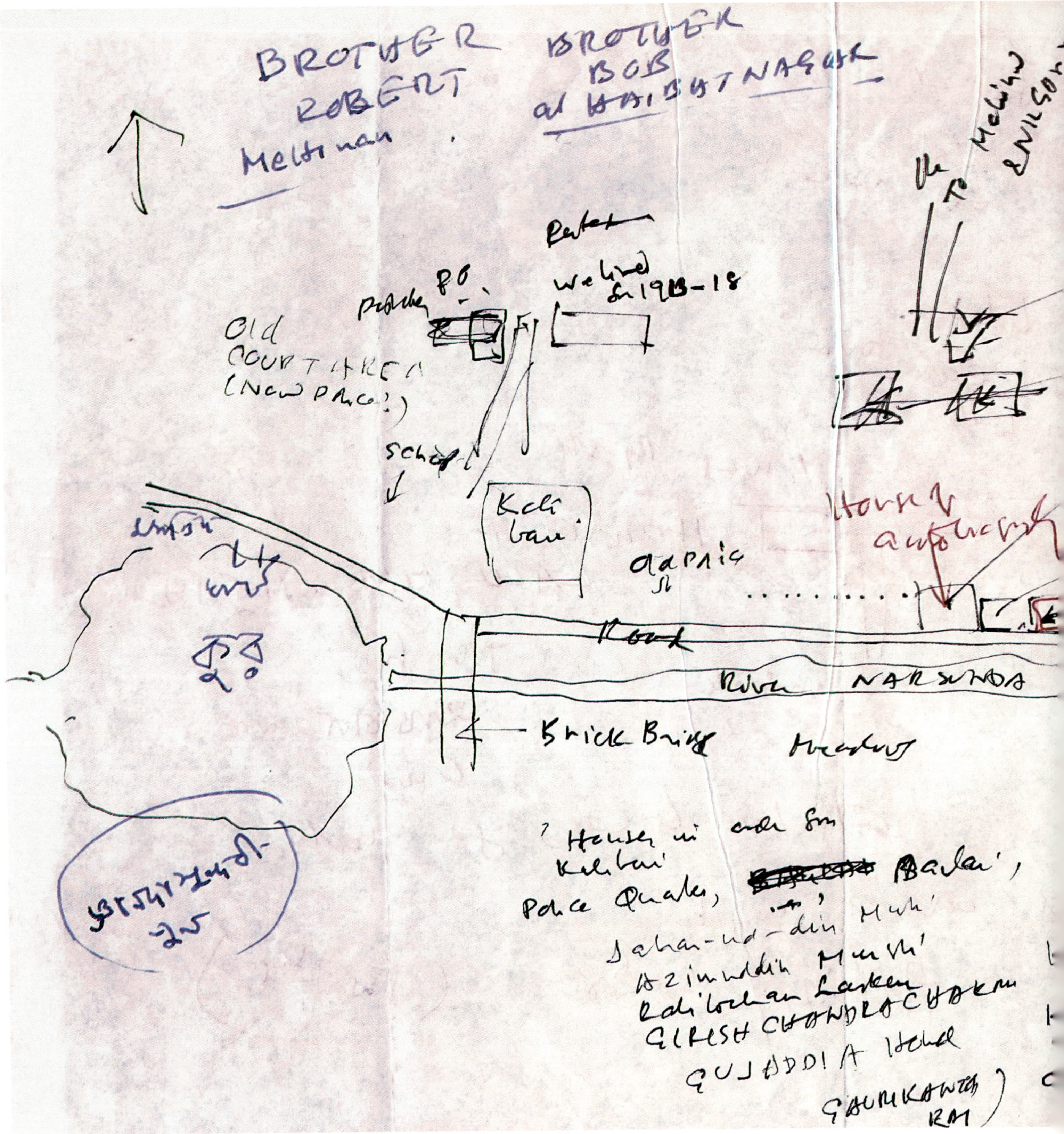
BROTHER
ROBERT
BROTHER
BOB
Old
COURT AREA
(NEW PALACE?)
Kali
bari
Brick Bridge

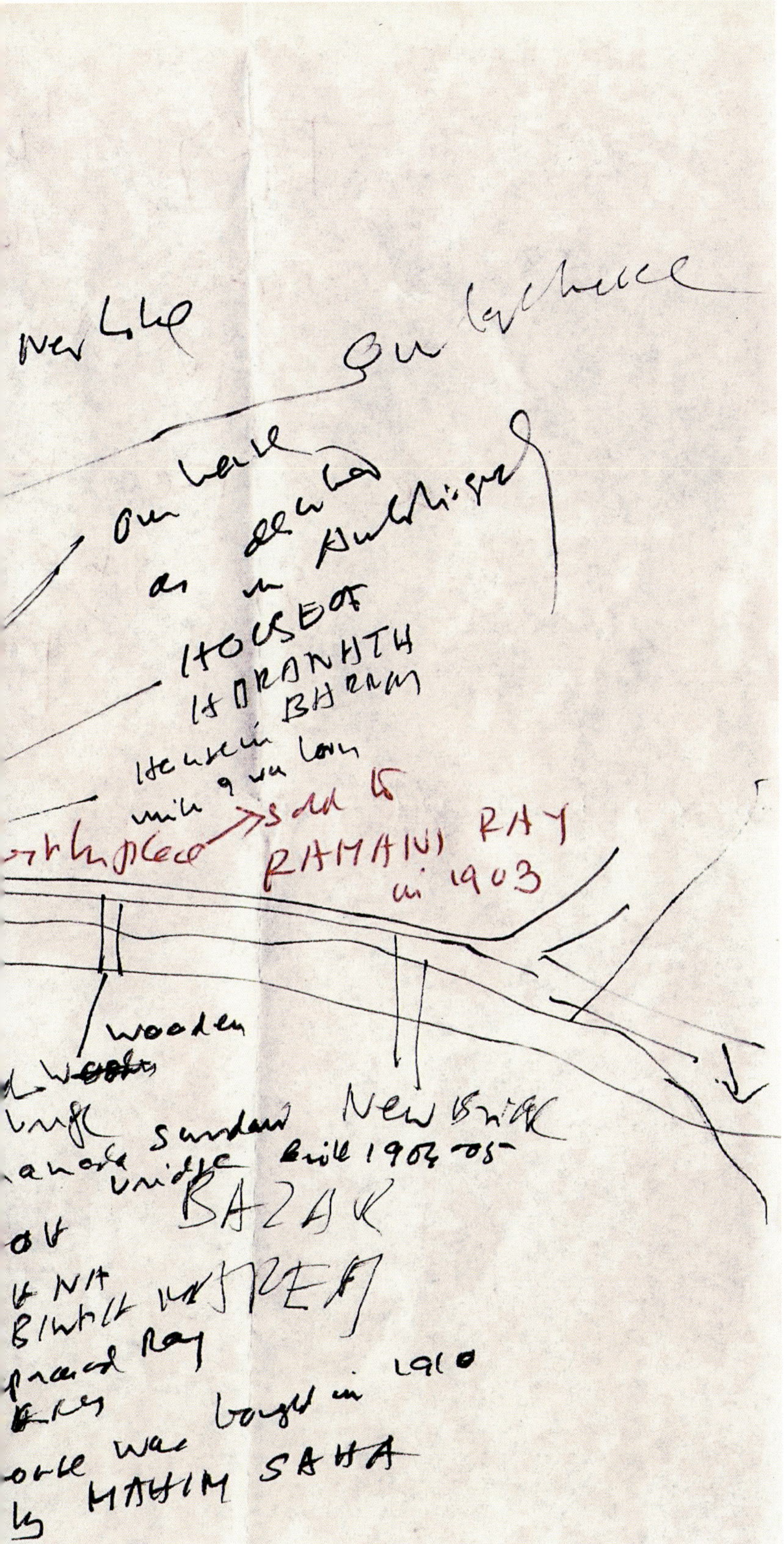

built with reed mats fixed to a solid wooden framework. Galvanised iron sheets were used for the roofs. As for the plinths and the floors, they were beaten earthwork, which needed to be wiped with a mixture of wet clay and cow dung cakes at regular intervals. This was the general pattern of houses in most small towns of East Bengal. To make his point visually clear, Father began to sketch the rough layout of their Kishorganj house; he also drew a map of the town. While he was doing this, I brought in some of my recent photographs taken in Agartala, the state capital of Tripura, bordering Bangladesh. The similarities between the two towns were obvious.

Having looked closely at the photographs, Father got really excited, particularly about the appearance of the reed huts that resembled those of Kishorganj and also over the pictures of lakes and rivers along with different types of country boats. Many of my photographs, he said, took him straight back to his early days. He related how there was a small river that used to flow from the River Brahmaputra, and divided Kishorganj into two. That river was only an emaciated stream during the summer and winter months. However, at the time of the monsoons it swelled up into a deep waterway. Boats of all sizes and shapes floated down

Hand-drawn map of Kishorganj, which Nirad Chaudhuri made to explain the location of his house.

the river and often moored at Kishorganj. They were the main mode of transport for people as well as goods. These boats also provided a comfortable way of visiting Banagram, which lay at a distance of about ten kilometres.

The railways did not reach Nirad Chaudhuri's birthplace till 1916. The steam engine puffing into the Kishorganj station was an awe-inspiring sight for many people, including two of my uncles who were just young boys then. But, neither the lack of communication and transport nor the remote location of Kishorganj affected the basic standard of life, including education, of the middle class who prospered in that sub-divisional town. My grandfather always went in for the best household items including non-electric light fittings. He introduced aluminium utensils and the kerosene stove for cooking in his house. As for the level of education and culture, Father told me of an incident that happened when he was a young boy of around ten. He was running along the riverbank loudly shouting out Nelson's battle signal used at Waterloo when a local *zamindar*, riding on an elephant, heard him. The *zamindar* was greatly impressed, and later said so to my grandfather. Though only a matriculate, my

This typical scene of Tripura is similar to what East Bengal looked like before 1947.

A typical East Bengal landscape with huts, which reminded Nirad Chaudhuri of his early days in Kishorganj, where he was born. His father had shifted from Banagram to this small town to pursue his career.

grandfather had a deep interest in English history and literature and this very much influenced the family.

Our conversation progressed. Father picked up a red pen and a scrap pad and drew our family tree, going back to his great-grandfather Kirti Narayan Chaudhuri, after whom my younger brother is named. He then took out two recent photographs of our distant relatives still living in Kishorganj and Banagram. The photographs were taken by Brother Robert from a Christian mission located at Mymensingh town in Bangladesh.

He also fished out another old photograph from a battered attaché case under his chair. That particular picture, rather yellowed with age and tattered, showed two reed cottages next to a pond, a typical village scene from East Bengal. It might have been taken by one of Nirad Chaudhuri's uncles, an amateur photographer who came from

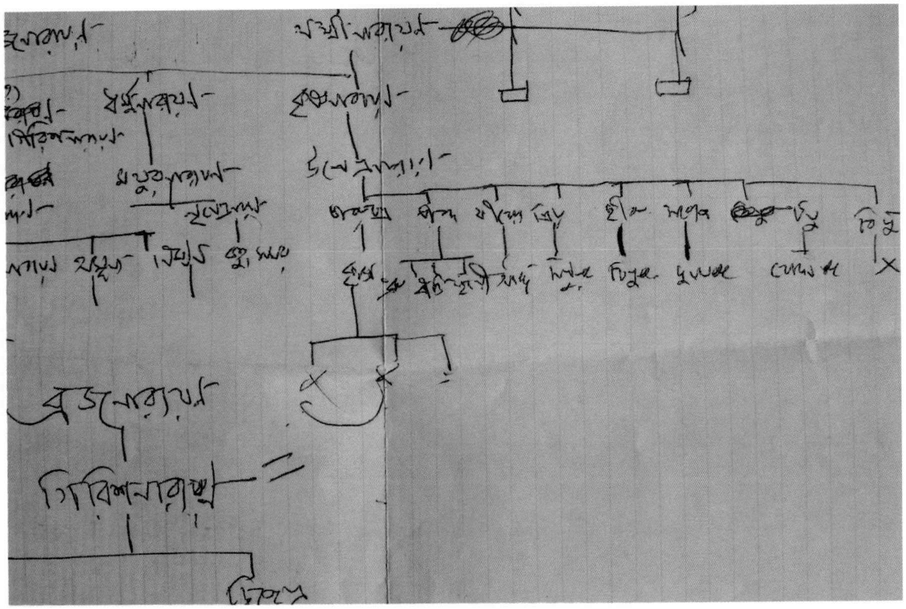

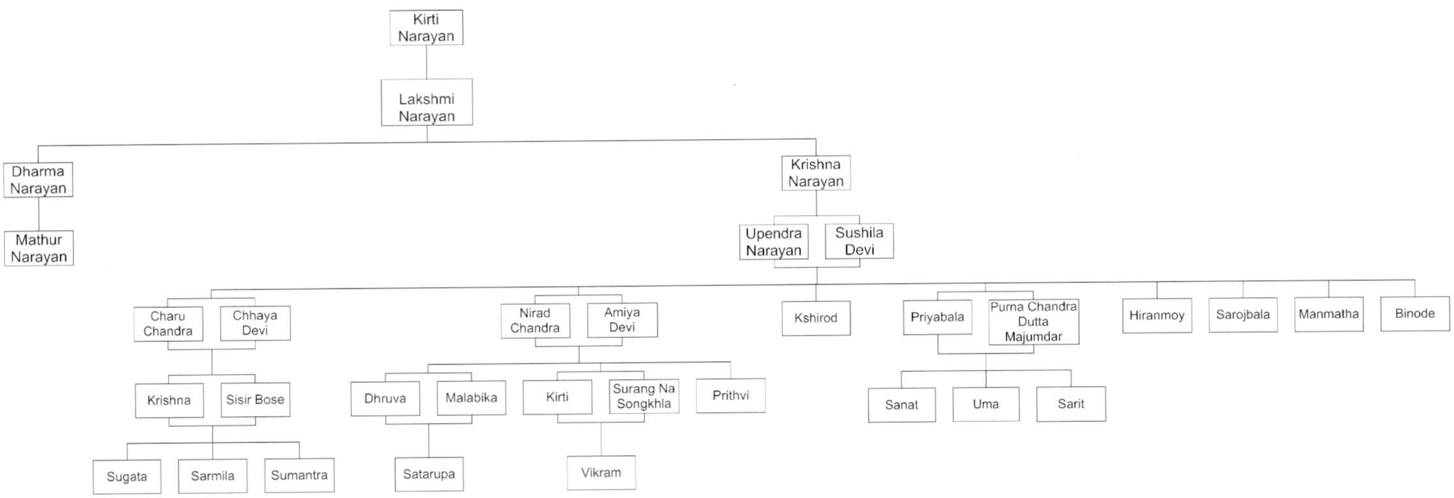

Above: A family tree illustrated by Nirad Chaudhuri using a red pen, in Bengali. Below is a translation by the author.

Kalikutch. After allowing me to keep that picture for inclusion in a documentary film I was working on, Father began to tell me about Banagram from the times of my great-grandfather.

Kirti Narayan, though head of the Chaudhuri family in Banagram, had a serious dispute about the family properties with his siblings and nephews. He finally left the ancestral house and set up an altogether new establishment called Notun Bari (New House), also located in Banagram. This division happened long ago, probably at the time of a local Pathan ruler called Murshid Quli Khan, after whom the town Murshidabad in West Bengal was named. Notun Bari became the home of Father's ancestors and though my grandfather had moved to Kishorganj, he along with his family visited Banagram often for weddings in the family or for religious festivals such as Durga Puja.

While relating all this, Father suddenly asked me about an antique hand bell that he had left behind in Delhi, which had an interesting anecdote attached to it. This bell, with a statue of Garuda on top, was used for his daily worship by Krishna Narayan Chaudhuri, my great-grandfather. The rice for his midday meal had to be cooked to an exact degree of softness. My great-grandmother timed the cooking with the ringing of this bell during worship and hence could prepare the rice perfectly. This prevented an outburst of temper, quite common among feudal husbands of Banagram.

Apart from the daily worship and rituals followed for the family deity, Gopinath, the annual festival of Durga Puja, held in autumn, was a grand occasion at Notun Bari. Durga Puja has now become like a community festival among Bengalis everywhere. But,

Ancestral bell and brass lamp from Banagram. The bell was used by Nirad Chaudhuri's grandfather for his prayers.

A nostalgic moment...talking about his early days in East Bengal, 1997.

according to Father, Durga Puja in his ancestral village was strictly a family affair. Whatever might have been the financial constraints affecting the Chaudhuris, this annual worshipping of Mother Durga was an important family obligation as well as a time of celebration and good cheer.

An exclusive Durga Puja at our ancestral home did not mean that the other families of Banagram were not welcome. As a matter of fact, my grandfather's eldest cousin Mathur Narayan Chaudhuri, who happened to be the head of the Chaudhuri family at the time, expected everyone from the village, including his Muslim tenants and farmers, to join the celebrations, which went on for at least five days. Sometimes Muslim farmers brought in many offerings for the Goddess even in the form of sacrificial animals such as goats. Many musicians, who played instruments such as the *shehnai*, violins and drums all through the festival days, often belonged to the Muslim community.

After finishing a cup of coffee and munching on a couple of biscuits, Nirad Chaudhuri went on to describe the evening *arati* during the Durga Pujas. At that ceremony, the aged family priest would lead the evening worship of Mother Durga, a heavy five-pointed brass lamp in one hand and bell in the other. On either side of the Goddess stood the married ladies of the family, all dressed in colourful silk *saris* and gold ornaments. It was only at the time of the *arati* that these ladies could show their faces to the outer world and, for the many young men assembled here, it would be a time that they had been eagerly waiting for!

'To pass from Banagram to my mother's village Kalikatchha or Kalikutch was to pass into a world so different, so humble, so full of humility and so self-effacing in bamboo and cane greenery that it brought tears to one's eyes,' wrote Nirad Chaudhuri about his mother's village in the famous book *The Autobiography of an Unknown Indian*. Along with his mother and siblings, Father used to visit Kalikutch almost every year from 1904 to 1909.

Boats in East Bengal, referred to by Nirad Chaudhuri in his writings in both Bengali and English.

Kalikutch was located in a district called Tipperah, now in Bangladesh. It was about five miles from the steamer station of Ajabpur on the River Meghna. While visiting my grandmother's village, the family of Upendra Narayan had to take a carriage or a boat (depending on the state of the river in Kishorganj) and then a steamer up to Ajabpur. The last stretch of five miles over land had to be covered by ladies and young children cooped up in a palanquin; for men and boys it could be nothing better than a brisk walk.

Distant relatives of the Chaudhuri family, who still live in Banagram. Photograph by Brother Robert.

According to Father, whatever the mode chosen to reach Kalikutch, there was no escaping a certain amount of discomfort. However, the rivers and large stretches of water of East Bengal would leave a deep impression on Nirad Chaudhuri's mind and would later find expression in many of his writings both in English and Bengali. I could only realise the depth of Father's feelings for large rivers and lakes when I visited Bangladesh and the State of Tripura.

Moving on with the story of his mother's family and Kalikutch, Nirad Chaudhuri mentioned that his maternal uncle, or Mama as he is usually called in Bengal, had to struggle hard as a government servant working in Shillong. Finally, after retiring as a deputy magistrate in 1909, he settled down in his own village to indulge in his favourite hobbies—photography and the cultivation of orchids, collected from the jungles of Khasi Hills all around Shillong.

Father ended the story of his early days with the description of two folk festivals celebrated all over East Bengal. They were known as Jhulan Mela and Rath Yatra, both held during the rainy season of July and August. Though these festivals were essentially Hindu in nature, people from both the Hindu and Muslim communities took part in the festivities, which included the buying and selling of all kinds of objects such as glassware, statues and even violins.

Nirad Chaudhuri looking out of the window, Lathbury Road, Oxford.

Just as we were discussing Jhulan Mela and Rath Yatra, Father realised that it was time for lunch—an early one—and he asked me to prepare a typical Bengali meal of *bhate bhat*, a combination of rice, boiled eggs, potatoes and some lentils, grocery items that I had ordered over the telephone. It did not take me long to cook this using an electric cooker and it was heart-warming to see him enjoying the meal, which must have been the usual brunch in Kishorganj or Banagram. While on the topic of eating eggs, Father related an interesting story about the eating preferences of my late grandfather Upendra Narayan. In Kishorganj, when the daily fare of rice, lentils, along with vegetables or fish, became commonplace, Upen Babu would ask one of his elder sons to go to a neighbouring Muslim eatery and fetch some spicy-hot egg curry along with a couple of crisp *bakarkhani rotis*. As food bought from a Muslim shop was usually taboo with their Hindu neighbours, this operation had to be done quietly at night under the cover of darkness.

It was an interesting juxtaposition to see Nirad Chaudhuri sitting at the table of his Victorian dining-room decorated with classical china and paintings, relishing a Bengali brunch. Indeed, I could not help but wonder how fate, destiny or what may be called determination had drawn Nirad C. Chaudhuri from the remote town of Kishorganj and the villages of Banagram and Kalikutch to a city of such great learning as Oxford in England, a place and a country he had only dreamt of during his childhood days in East Bengal.

Call of the City

St Paul's Cathedral in Calcutta...according to Nirad Chaudhuri, the city closely resembled London.

My grandfather decided to move to Calcutta (now called Kolkata) with his entire family in June 1910. This decision, according to Father, was the result of many factors including symptoms of a grave illness that my grandmother was suspected to be suffering from. She had bouts of bad mental health apart from which doctors in Kishorganj thought that she might have cancer. Among the other reasons for this shift was a constant upheaval faced in their daily lives, including in that of the education of the older boys, due to the freedom movement having taken a violent turn, particularly in East Bengal.

Calcutta at that time was the capital of India and Viceroys or Governor Generals lived in the Government House next to Eden Gardens, facing Fort William, the first stronghold of British India. While the Viceregal Lodge was modelled after Kedleston Hall, the ancestral house of Lord Curzon, the Writer's Building, which housed and still houses the main government offices, was built following the Renaissance style of French architecture. The other landmark of Calcutta, the High Court, once again still in use, was built like the Cloth Hall at Ypres in Belgium.

Father proceeded with a description of old Calcutta as seen from the rooftop of

The Calcutta skyline fascinated Nirad Chaudhuri who used to admire it from the terrace.

their Serpentine Lane house. However, he digressed slightly to mention an interesting, or rather an awkward incident, which happened on the very first day of their reaching the capital, while they were trying to find their way to the house in Serpentine Lane. This particular lane, especially towards the end where it touched Bow Bazaar Street, happened to be a locality inhabited by sex workers. Since the coachman bringing Father and some of his brothers from the railway station had no idea about this lane, he kept stopping at every doorstep. Many women of various age groups rushed out, only to scream, 'Oh no!' The sight of some young and rustic looking boys sitting in a hackney carriage must have disappointed them.

Talking about their house, Father recollected that when they climbed up to the terrace above the third floor they could see a number of church spires and, in spite of the shabby rooftops visible all around, the city had a strong visual resemblance to London.

Though Calcutta was called the City of Palaces from the time of Fanny Parks in 1822, Nirad Chaudhuri could appreciate the full significance of that attribute only years later when he sailed down the River Hooghly in a steam launch to visit the Botanical Gardens. The façade, which impressed Father, was a row of impressive buildings such as the Whiteway & Ladlow Store, the Indian Museum, and even

St Paul's Cathedral, visible near the famous Chowringhee. Behind these buildings lay the European locality comprising Wood Street, Camac Street and Elysium Row, which had huge bungalows with gardens and stood on roads planted with rows of flowering trees. Among the large domes visible at the time, the white dome of the General Post Office at Dalhousie Square, it seems, was the most prominent. Years later, the Victoria Memorial would come to occupy that place. However, in 1910, that impressive marble building was still under construction and the five large cranes used for this purpose would appear like a panoramic etching done by the English artist Sir Frank William Brangwyn.

Behind the rows of European quarters was the locality inhabited by Indians, mostly Bengalis. This area was not only somewhat dingy but the roads and streets had beaten earth on their surfaces and during the rainy season were extremely unpleasant to walk upon. It was only after 1924, when the Calcutta Corporation began to be controlled by prominent Congress leaders such as C.R. Das and Subhas Chandra Bose, that these roads improved and came to have asphalt coating.

Facing page: Always well-dressed and dynamic, Nirad Chaudhuri, at the age of ninety, stepping out, for his weekly shopping.

Father observed that despite the congestion and squalor in these traditional Bengali quarters, leading figures such as Bankim Chandra Chatterji, Kesab Chandra Sen, Vidya Sagar and even the family of Rabindranath Tagore preferred to live in such localities. They seldom moved to the luxury and quietness of Park Street, Theatre Road or even the Lower Circular Road.

For my grandparents the dream of settling down in Calcutta did not last for more than three years. Though my grandmother was free from the danger of having cancer, my grandfather's business venture of running a cycle shop ended as a failure owing to a sudden complication in his health, which needed surgery. So while the family were to return to Banagram, Nirad Chaudhuri, along with his eldest brother Charu Chandra Chaudhuri, would remain in Calcutta for their education. They stayed at a privately run hostel, referred to in those days as a mess. It was located at 128 Amherst Street, once again in the central part of Calcutta.

A year later, after passing the school final (or the Matriculation) examination, Father began to attend Ripon College for his First Arts examination. He moved to the Oxford Mission Hostel along with his elder brother. Their hostel superintendent was an English clergyman called Father Prior who, despite the rather awkward appearance and manners of my father as a teenager, encouraged him to go through the volumes of the *Encyclopaedia Britannica*, a habit that Nirad Chaudhuri retained right up to his old age.

A student's life in those days was certainly different, recalled Father. For example, it was impossible to remain aloof from the freedom struggle or from the revolutionaries of Bengal for that matter. As for academics, at all levels including in schools, very few students read merely for passing an examination. Soon after joining college and attending lectures by the historian Bipin Gupta, Father was convinced that history would be his Honours subject and an academic life his career.

However, destiny had other plans for Nirad C. Chaudhuri. He joined Scottish Church College for his B.A. degree with history as the main subject and secured a first division. But he found himself ill prepared for the M.A. final examination and, later that year, after a half-hearted attempt to resume his studies, Father, once a brilliant student, abandoned his original idea of becoming a university professor.

The reason for this academic failure, according to Nirad Chaudhuri himself, was not difficult to guess. He had gone completely overboard reading many

By the side of the River Ganges in Calcutta, the city where Nirad Chaudhuri studied.

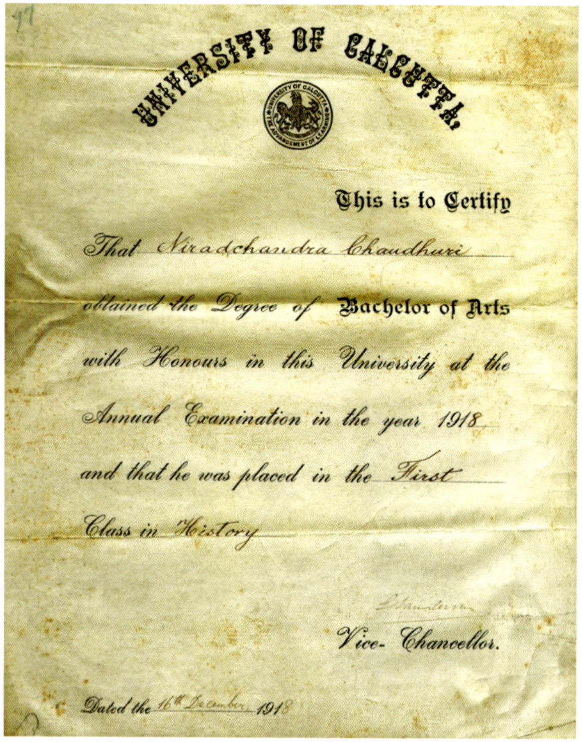

UNIVERSITY OF CALCUTTA.

This is to Certify

That Niradchandra Chaudhuri

obtained the Degree of Bachelor of Arts

with Honours in this University at the

Annual Examination in the year 1918

and that he was placed in the First

Class in History

Vice-Chancellor.

Dated the 16th December 1918

Bachelor of Arts degree conferred on Nirad Chaudhuri by the University of Calcutta, 1918.

historians such as Titus Livius and Albert Sorel in French, the language that he had taught himself, the prescribed course of the university got neglected and hence it was impossible to cope with the entire course at the time of his final examination.

For his father, too, there were many disappointments in store. After returning to Kishorganj from Calcutta my grandfather would manage to build a flourishing legal practice once again, he would also manage to build a proper brick house for the first time in his life. But the building would collapse in the severe earthquake of 1917. That calamity —along with his wife's constant ill health, and later Father's failure at the M.A. examination —left him sad, but still enthusiastic about supporting the academic career of a most promising son. However, Father squandered the money received for his studies in buying expensive books and clothes for himself and, when he finally returned to Kishorganj, he had to face the silent but strong disapproval of his father. Nirad Chaudhuri, instead of waiting for an improvement in his father's mood, decided to try his luck in Calcutta once again. After a few futile and depressing weeks in the late summer of 1921, which he spent reading at the Imperial Library, he finally got a clerical job at the Military Accounts Department of the Government of India through the intervention of one of his elder cousins who held a senior post there.

The starting salary was fabulous for those days, a full hundred rupees a month. Father faced the challenges of his job with utmost seriousness. His superior officer, an English colonel, was impressed with Nirad Chaudhuri's writing of English prose on as prosaic a subject as a senior military officer's transport claim. The words of appreciation from the officer spread fast and, within a few months, Father was promoted to assistant superintendent.

Nirad Chaudhuri enjoyed talking about his early days to Satarupa, his granddaughter, 1991.

At that time, Father stayed at a boarding house at 41 Mirzapur Street in central Calcutta. Apart from his younger brother, who was studying to be a doctor at the Calcutta Medical College, the other person at the lodging was Bibhuti Bhushan Banerji. He had been Father's batchmate at Ripon College and would become well-known after writing *Pather Panchali*, a novel that was made into a classic film by the legendary Satyajit Ray many years later. The first few pages of this novel were read by Father while they were living at this lodging and later recommended to Sajani Kanta Das, a journalist and also a publisher.

Taking a break from his writings, Nirad Chaudhuri reading with great concentration about Calcutta.

The job at the Military Accounts Department went on well for about six months; but the routine nature of the work became rather frustrating for an innovative and creative person such as Nirad Chaudhuri. He became indifferent and slack. Nonetheless his name was proposed for a departmental examination in order to confirm his early ad hoc promotion. He was also granted a two-month preparatory leave in 1922 and advised to study the various rulebooks and account manuals used by the department.

No less than seventy years later, Nirad Chaudhuri admitted in one of his articles written for *Desh* that he went nowhere near those rulebooks and manuals. Instead, he took up the reading of various classics of English literature in earnest and, in particular, a poet called Matthew Arnold. Though Father was familiar with some of the essays and other prose writings of Matthew Arnold, the poem titled 'Scholar Gypsy' had completely escaped his attention earlier. Fascinated by the rhetoric and the subject matter of the poem for years, Nirad Chaudhuri quoted this passage in his article in *Desh*:

> Thou hast not liv'd, why should'st
> thou perish, so?
>
> Thou hadst one aim, one business,
> one desire;
>
> ...and we,
>
> Light half-believers of our
> casual creeds,
>
> Who never deeply felt, nor
> clearly will'd
>
> Whose insight never has borne
> fruit in deeds,
>
> Whose vague resolves never have
> been fulfilled;
>
> For whom each year we see
>
> Breeds new beginnings,
> disappointments new;
>
> Who hesitate and falter life away,
>
> And lose tomorrow the
> ground won today…'

Inspired by these words, Father wanted to turn himself into a scholar gypsy. The first step in that direction was his decision to give up his job. However, it was necessary to wait till his brother, who was financially dependent on him, finished his course. The immediate casualty of that headstrong decision was the proposed departmental examination.

To escape the frequent reprimands from his superiors and also taunts from his office colleagues, Nirad Chaudhuri wrote an article on 'Civilisation in India'. It was a detailed criticism of the research done by Lord Ronaldshay, once the Governor of Bengal, on the cause of the Indian unrest. It was published in *The Statesman*, a leading newspaper in Calcutta run by English staff. Though this article did not have his byline because of government regulations, it was noticed in the literary circles of Calcutta. Some even went to the extent of attributing it to a noted scholar and author, Bipin Chandra Pal. Father then went on to write about an eighteenth century Bengali poet, Bharat Chandra, who belonged to the popular Vaishnavite sect. This article, once again in English, was written at the suggestion of Mohitlal Majumdar, who had once been Father's teacher, and at that point in time was his literary mentor. It was Ramananda Chatterjee, a well-respected editor and social reformer, also close to Rabindranath Tagore, who printed this

EDWARDVS VII
REX IMPERATOR

article in *Modern Review*, an influential periodical of those days.

Father was fed up with the general work culture in his office and asked for a transfer. This request was sanctioned in no time and he was told to report to the accounts department of the explosive factory in Kirkee, near Pune. But, on the eve of his departure from Calcutta, Father received the news that his mother had once again had a stroke; she died before he could reach Kishorganj. This tragic event left Father in an inconsolable frame of mind. He began to frequent the cremation ground called Neemtala Ghat near his office; he even wrote a story bearing the same name. The particular story was about a young clerk called Sudhir, who had to attend the funeral of a colleague at Neemtala Ghat. Some of his colleagues wanted to have a good time despite the melancholy occasion; they also tried their best to make money out of the funeral expenses to be paid by the office, controlled by a British officer. Sudhir was more or less a personification of Father, who felt he was a total misfit among his colleagues, and was also obsessed with the idea of death. This inconclusive story was not published and, after the manuscript had survived sixty years of neglect, it was included in the book *Thy Hand, Great Anarch!*

Finally, in 1926, Nirad Chaudhuri resigned from government service. A clash of opinion with his superior officer against a transfer

Facing page: Victoria Memorial, Calcutta, the city where Nirad Chaudhuri went to nurture his dream of becoming a writer. Above left to right: A print from a monograph on cave paintings and a Medici print—Nirad Chaudhuri used to indulge himself by buying beautiful works of art on credit.

order was the reason for precipitating this crisis. After spending the arrears of his salary in buying a full-size Medici print of Leonardo da Vinci's Mona Lisa, and having it framed in expensive mahogany wood, he escaped to Benares as an escort to an old widow, a relative of his elder sister-in-law. This opportunity was eagerly taken not only because Father wanted to see the ancient Hindu city, but also in order to avoid the frequent taunts from his siblings and many friends.

On his return from an idyllic visit to Benares, including Sarnath, Nirad Chaudhuri's habit of buying on credit rare books, monographs on cave paintings and prints of old masters such as Botticelli, led to several unpleasant incidents as well as financial squabbles with his siblings. One day such an acrimony among the brothers reached a point of no return. Father, after wandering all day without food, spent a good part of the night hiding in an empty carriage at the Sealdah railway yard. This resulted in high fever and delirium due to exhaustion. My grandfather had to rush down to Calcutta in order to save his second son from further trouble and within a few days he took Nirad back to Kishorganj.

A Writer at Last

Lost in the world of music, Nirad Chaudhuri listening to operas, identifying songs heard first in Calcutta.

Towards the end of November 1927 Nirad Chaudhuri left Kishorganj for Calcutta to realise his cherished aspiration of becoming a writer. As for a plan, or an expectation about the future, Father was even more uncertain and vague than in 1921 when he had reached Calcutta to look for a job. This time, as expressed in *Thy Hand, Great Anarch!*, he had no intention to search for a regular job. Some form of a literary career was the only option open to him and for that it was imperative to live in Calcutta.

Father's journey from Kishorganj to Calcutta, the last that he was to undertake in this direction, was completed in a better frame of mind than in 1921. There were two reasons for that change—the clearing up of the tension that had developed between his father and him and, second, the success of his first Bengali article published in a magazine called *Sanibarer Chithi* (Saturday Letter). The proposal to write for this magazine, well-known for its socio-political satires, had come from Mohitlal Majumdar, who introduced him to a Bengali literary group in Calcutta.

A group of friends led by Sajani Kanta Das, who was known for his humorous style of writing, had begun to revive *Sanibarer*

Office of The Modern Review *and* Prabasi *in Calcutta, where Nirad Chaudhuri used to work.*

Chithi. Father had written for the first issue under the pen name Balahawk Nandi, which in Bengali means clouds, same as Nirad, and Nandi is the name of our sub-caste. Father was offered the editorship of this magazine soon after reaching Calcutta. With his incisive editorial style *Sanibarer Chithi* became an important magazine among the intellectuals of Calcutta. But in less than a year's time, some of the writings by others, bordering on the obscene, quoted by Sajani Kanta Das in *Sanibarer Chithi* to increase its circulation, had invited trouble from the office of the Police Commissioner of Calcutta. Father was warned at the police headquarters in Lal Bazar and he resigned as the editor.

After a few months of idling and turning once again to the charity of his brothers, particularly the one who had become a doctor, Nirad Chaudhuri joined *The Modern Review* and its Bengali counterpart *Prabasi*, owned and edited by Ramananda Chatterjee, as the assistant editor. This sudden stroke of luck came his way again because of Mohit Babu who had come to know from Ashoke Chatterjee, one of Ramananda Babu's sons, that an editorial person was required for *The Modern Review.* He had then promptly recommended Father.

It was while Nirad Chaudhuri was spending his time idling away at his doctor brother's house on Harrison Road, now known as Mahatma Gandhi Road, that he was struck

by his first infatuation. Right across that road lived a family with two young girls aged around fifteen and seventeen, respectively. According to what he wrote in *Thy Hand, Great Anarch!*, both these girls became the centre of attention whenever they came up to the terrace for some fresh air, combined with the task of collecting washed and dried clothes, a standard practice among middle class families of Calcutta. Father compared the look and bearings of the elder girl to that of a violin being played in the vibrato. In the next paragraph there is a frank confession: 'I fell head over heels in love with that vision… but made no attempts to be introduced to her family. I never came to know who she was. I worshipped her with my eyes, without giving the impression of staring or even watching.' Soon, with his brother going abroad for studies, Father had to leave that large house. He, however, made no attempt to see the girl again or return to the same locality.

Father felt quite at ease working as an assistant editor, and his salary—like his first job–was hundred rupees a month. But that amount was never regular and usually paid in dribbles of rupees five or ten. Yet, in spite of these financial uncertainties, Nirad Chaudhuri went on working for the two magazines because of their reputation. It is said that even the British governors and the Indian Civil Service officers read *The Modern Review*. As for *Prabasi*, no Bengali household was considered educated if it did not subscribe to that magazine.

The other reason for carrying on with Ramananda Chatterjee's magazines was the fact that Nirad Chaudhuri had turned into a nationalist and an ardent supporter of Mahatma Gandhi and his non-cooperation movement. Besides writing articles with a strong nationalist expression, Father took up *khadi* as dress material and also sandalwood soap and Indian toiletries for daily use. He even went to the extent of walking to Salt Lake to witness the defiant salt making that was led by a follower of Mahatma Gandhi, S.C. Das Gupta.

It was during this phase of his life that Father met an unusual Englishman, Christopher Ackroyd, who was a lecturer of history at St Paul's College. Ackroyd usually wore Bengali attire made from *khadi*. He had written a pamphlet about the communal problems that occurred after the Chittagong Armoury Raid in 1931. Europeans in Calcutta wanted to have him expelled from the college and sent back to England. However, this conspiracy to expel him got exposed when a letter from the European Association, along with the one from Father, got printed in the nationalist paper *Amrita Bazaar Patrika* of Calcutta.

Facing page: A thoughtful Nirad Chaudhuri in Oxford, going back in time to write about his working life in Calcutta. After leaving Kishorganj in 1927, he had started his career as a journalist.

A glimpse of an old house in Calcutta, facing a busy street, similar to the days when Nirad Chaudhuri lived here.

Ackroyd had to go on leave to England. He asked Father to keep his gramophone along with many records of European classical music and listen to them at leisure.

Though everyone in Nirad Chaudhuri's family, including my grandmother, followed a musical tradition in their houses, the pastime was mostly confined to the singing of what is now called Tagore songs. Even among those songs written and music composed by Rabindranath Tagore the emphasis was on songs with a devotional theme. Father's first contact with European music was largely theoretical and confined to what he had read mostly in novels such as *The Kreutzer Sonata* by Leo Tolstoy and Romain Rolland's *Jean-Christophe*. His first experience of listening to classical European music happened at a Calcutta bookshop owned by a friend. Recalling that particular day in

1930, Father remembers seeing a portable (hand-wound) gramophone along with three record albums (78 rpm) lying on a counter. Soon, the owner of the shop, along with a stranger who appeared to have returned from Europe, began to play some of those records. Father, while turning over the pages of some newly-arrived books, became totally engrossed in listening to the music. Fifty years later, he told friends in Oxford that those records were early recordings by operatic singers such as Amelita Galli-Curci.

Not only did Nirad Chaudhuri get hooked to the songs of Schubert, Brahms and Korsakov, he also realised that the female operatic singers from the West had a quality that could never be compared to his childhood myth of 'howling like a jackal'. To keep up with his new-found infatuation with European music, Father would then borrow records from his friends.

Ackroyd's records and gramophone provided Father with the impetus for going deeper into the world of European classical music. He soon realised that it was not enough just to listen to the music, even with a musical score in hand. The famous musicologist Percy Alfred Scholes through his book *Listener's Guide to Music* emerged as a pathfinder and rescued him from a literal drowning into the depths of the world of Western classical music.

Nirad Chaudhuri's father, Upendra Narayan Chaudhuri, was given the task of finding a bride for him.

However, there was a not so pleasant side to Nirad Chaudhuri's deep involvement with listening to this kind of music. My eldest uncle, many of Father's literary friends, including close ones such as Bibhuti Babu, could just not understand this infatuation, which, according to them, perhaps bordered on the point of madness. The result was that from the early thirties, Father had to live practically alone at Bagbazar, a locality in dingy North Calcutta. Only two of his youngest brothers would give him company from time to time. That, too, ended when they were arrested for being freedom fighters and sent to jail by the police of Calcutta. Even Father's rooms and books were searched, but he managed to hoodwink the police by scratching out the titles of the army manuals he had and used to write articles on army training in India. At that time, Father was in touch with Pandit Jawaharlal Nehru, whom he had met through his colleague Pandit Banarasi Das Chaturvedi, a noted figure in the world of Hindi journalism. Some of those letters written by Father to Pandit Nehru came to be intercepted by the police and are still preserved at the National Archives of New Delhi.

In November 1931, four years after his return to Calcutta from Kishorganj, Nirad Chaudhuri began to feel dejected and alone. No amount of listening to his favourite music helped uplift his mood. His idea of having a love marriage vanished after his failure to follow up on his infatuation with the two girls of the neighbourhood where he lived. Years later, in one of his Bengali articles and during a television interview for Doordarshan, he attributed that failure to his unimpressive appearance and also the lack of moral courage to pursue his feelings in such matters.

Finally, my grandfather was approached to find a suitable bride for Father and that request was welcomed by all, including my eldest uncle. Father left the entire business of the selection and arranging the marriage to his relatives and he was mentally prepared to even give up his obsession for Western music if desired by his bride. But when asked about the intellectual level of the bride-to-be by his Father, he tapped his forehead and replied in English that there was enough for two in there.

A Suitable Bride

Amiya Dhar, 1928—four years before she got married to Nirad Chaudhuri.

The search for Nirad Chaudhuri's bride ended in February 1932.

As chance would have it, Mother, along with her parents, was staying in a flat right behind my aunt's (Father's younger sister's) house in Calcutta. It was the same aunt who had been looking for a bride for her brother. The match was arranged without Father seeing his future wife, Amiya Dhar, even once. According to a tradition in East Bengal, spouses of landlords with the title of Chaudhuri were known as Chaudhuranis. Nirad Chaudhuri, though progressive in many ways, believed in giving importance to his family traditions in more ways than one and so it was decided that Mother's surname would become Chaudhurani.

Amiya Dhar was born on 9 June 1909 in Shillong, a hill station and the capital of Assam during the British rule. My maternal grandfather, Rai Sahib Dinanath Dhar, was a well-respected government officer of the Shillong municipality. He had supervised the reconstruction of the Shillong town, including the restoration of the famous Wards Lake, after the severe earthquake in 1897. That earthquake had affected the entire north-east of India, shortly before Nirad Chaudhuri was born.

Mother was the third sister in the family and to my grandparents' great sorrow, her birthday coincided with the death of their only son at the age of two-and-half years. Though Mother's birthday was never celebrated in Shillong, her father tried to fulfil his ambition of giving a good education to his daughter by sending her first to a missionary school in Shillong and then to the Brahmo Girls School in Calcutta. After the school final examination she studied at the City College of Calcutta and later did her Intermediate in Arts from

Amiya Dhar's father, Rai Sahib Dinanath Dhar, who was from Shillong.

Scottish Church College. Right from her high school days to the end of the Intermediate examinations she stayed mostly in hostels and had a diverse experience of both British and *swadeshi* culture.

At the age of twelve, when Mother first came down to Calcutta for her eldest sister's wedding, she resented having to wear a sari instead of a frock. At the time of her marriage, when she was about to touch twenty-three, Amiya Dhar was a young lady who had attended two colleges; both were co-educational.

The wedding took place on 21 April 1932. A special building had been hired on a nearby street—Priya Nath Mullick Road. This building had a huge hall and spacious rooms with a large terrace. It was often rented for weddings and other functions. The reception, according to Mother, was a grand affair attended by literary luminaries such as Dr Suniti Kumar Chatterji, Bibhuti Bhusan Bannerji, Amol Home and of course Father's seniors and colleagues such as Kedar Chatterji. They were very generous and brought art objects, curios and their own books as gifts. Father's colleague and friend Ashoke Chatterjee, on seeing the bride, proudly announced that she was once his student at City College. Sajani Kanta Das received a verbal bashing from one of my grandfathers for clicking too many photographs of the bride.

A portrait of Nirad Chaudhuri by his friend, Parimal Goswamy, Calcutta.

Ten days after the wedding ceremony, my parents moved into a flat on the second floor of a building called Jatindra Mansion. This large block of many flats was located on the Upper Circular Road near the Shyam Bazaar market. A unique feature of my parents' new home was a building, across the street, which had a clock tower. One of the four clock-faces could always be seen from every room of the flat. So for the next eight years no timepiece could be found anywhere in our house. This clock tower and Jatindra Mansion still stand

Shyam Bazaar, Calcutta, where Nirad Chaudhuri lived in a flat on the second floor of Jatindra Mansion, opposite the clock tower.

A side view of the Shyam Bazaar flat, where Nirad Chaudhuri's three sons were born.

in Kolkata and I had the good fortune of photographing them in the last week of April 2006.

Many of the inhabitants of that building and also of that locality were rather surprised to see the new furniture, household items and stacks of books that were offloaded from a truck. In addition, most neighbours found Mother's style of dressing and her smart appearance unusual and began to refer to her rather sarcastically as a graduate housewife. An old man living across the street took to staring at her and once Mother had to actually slam a balcony door to escape his unwarranted attention.

The rent for this flat was rupees fifty a month, exactly half of Father's salary. Nirad Chaudhuri had no cash balance left after incurring the expenses of his marriage as well as setting up the new flat. So as a young bride Mother had to struggle hard to provide for the family, which included two freedom fighter brothers-in-law just released from the Dumdum Central Jail. In early 1934, about a year after I was born, Father resigned from *The Modern Review* after receiving only twelve *annas*, or three-quarters of a rupee, out of his salary of one hundred rupees. But within a short time he was offered the editorship of a new daily newspaper called *Free India*. His workload increased to the point of his having to neglect his young wife and baby boy. Nonetheless Father took up the challenge for the sake of a monthly salary of Rs 200 a month and a free telephone.

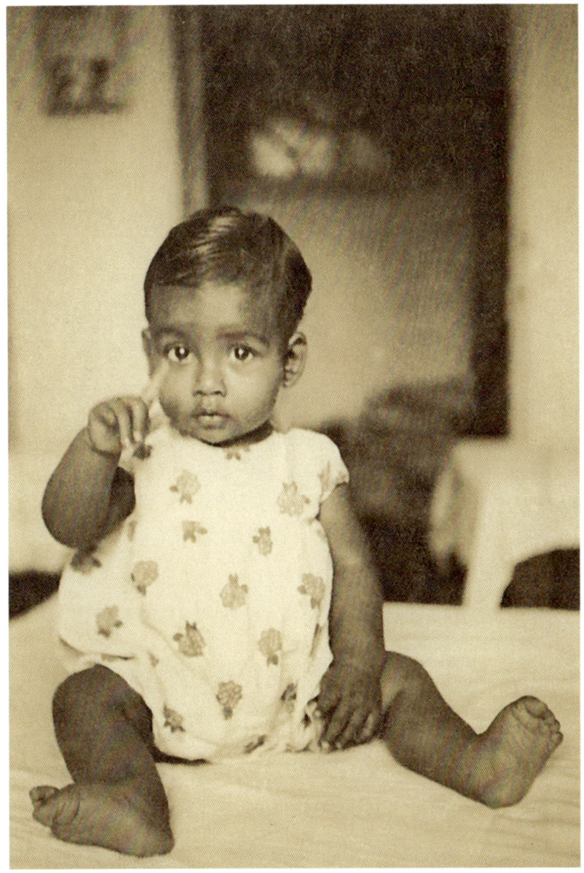

Author and photographer Dhruva N. Chaudhuri as a toddler, 1934-1935.

Facing page: Amiya with her son, Dhruva, the eldest of their three boys. The young mother had to struggle to provide for the family.

Spending a quiet moment at home with his wife and two sons, 1937. Photograph courtesy Parimal Goswamy.

Unfortunately, this paper folded up within a month or two and once again Nirad Chaudhuri was unemployed, with very little money to fall back upon. Despite the circumstances, he would not allow Mother to appear for her B.A. examination as a private candidate and take up a job as a school teacher. As a further shock to everyone in our family, my grandfather died of a stroke within a few hours of receiving the news that his second son was once again unemployed. My widower grandfather had moved to Benares shortly after the marriage of my parents. From that holy refuge he had sent a letter of reassurance to Father. And this letter, actually a postcard, arrived in Calcutta two days after my grandfather passed away.

It was a real difficult time for my parents. Nirad Chaudhuri mentions in some of his writings that often they went to bed with no money to buy provisions for the next morning. The only ray of hope was his youngest brother Binode Chandra Chaudhuri. Uncle Binu, as we children called him, was a confirmed bachelor and lived with us till we moved to Delhi. In fact, shortly before Father resigned from *The Modern Review* and *Prabasi* he had taught Uncle Binu how to correct proofs and supervise the printing of a magazine. After working as a non-paid apprentice for some time, Uncle was employed by the Prabasi Press for one rupee a day. I vaguely remember that it was my first duty in the morning to toddle to Uncle Binu's room and collect a one-rupee coin, the sole earnings of our family for some time.

End of the Beginning

Nirad Chaudhuri speaking for a 1982 BBC film about the difficult days spent in Calcutta.

Father had started his career as a journalist and writer after leaving Kishorganj in 1927. Seven years later, even after the publication of many well-appreciated articles and three editorships of reputed journals and a newspaper, there was no certainty about a regular monthly income. Father attributed this distressing experience to two important factors. The first was his attitude of being a rigid perfectionist in every area of his professional work. The second factor, which was equally important, was that Father would not tolerate any affront from anyone in a superior position.

Father carried on for a few months with some arrears and sureties he had received from Free India and then in sheer desperation went back to the Prabasi Press for the possibility of re-employment, only to face a refusal. For the sake of old times, Ashoke Chatterjee suggested that Nirad Chaudhuri should try his luck with the owners of a well-known press who were interested in bringing out a new magazine similar to *The Illustrated Weekly of India* from Calcutta. When Father went to see the eldest partner he was not only polite, but straightaway employed him as an editor. However, within a few weeks the younger of the owners, who was the manager of the printing press, made a disparaging remark

Bally or Willingdon Bridge, Calcutta, where seaplanes used to land, 1938-1939.

when Father asked him about some printing problems in the new magazine. Nirad Chaudhuri walked out of that job and did not even return to claim his legitimate dues.

It was around this time in September 1934 that my brother Kirti Narayan was born. The family was under extreme financial stress but fortunately Nirad Chaudhuri got an assignment from his friend Amal Home, the editor of *Calcutta Municipal Gazette*, to bring out a special issue to celebrate the silver jubilee of King George V. This work stretched far longer than the stipulated two months and Amal Home could do nothing to pay extra for the additional period. However, five rupees out of the small honorarium finally received was spent in buying me a set of building blocks from the English departmental store of Hall and Anderson's on Park Street. This, though important to Father but a so-called wasteful expenditure to others, was reported to my maternal grandmother who asked Father for an explanation!

Towards the end of 1935 there was a new hope for Nirad Chaudhuri in the form of an editorship of a weekly magazine called *Notun Patrika* (New Magazine). The proposal had come once again from Sajani Kanta Das, who was doing well as a publisher and printer. As the editor of the magazine, Father insisted on accepting only those written contributions that were of a high order and went on to print photographs with quality pictorial content

Woodburn Park, Sarat Chandra Bose's residence and Nirad Chaudhuri's office, 1937-1941.

in the best standard of halftone printing. However, this unique magazine folded up after bringing out only five issues. The sponsor, Kapil Bhattacharya, found the cost of production to be beyond all expectations and refused to finance the magazine any further. Nirad Chaudhuri had to then continue to earn some kind of living by editing or even ghost writing for scholars and authors of repute. But the one notable exception was a recommendation from Sir Jadunath Sarkar, the eminent historian who had guided Kunwar Raghuvir Singh of the Sitamau state to do a doctoral thesis on the history of the Malwa Rajputs. Father was asked to edit and revise this thesis for publishing it as a book. One day Kunwar Sahib came to our Shyam Bazaar flat and after a long discussion and drinking the tea served by Mother, he sent Rs 50 as an advance, which made Mother happy because she had the money at last to buy some sweets for us on Dussehra.

The year 1937 brought a certain peace of mind for Nirad Chaudhuri. The money he had earned by writing for others was to be adequate for the next couple of months. So, feeling somewhat in higher spirits after several years of financial trouble and anxiety, Father gladly accepted an invitation to preside over a Bengali literary conference to be held in Patna. Most of the delegates were from his circle of literary friends from *Sanibarer Chithi*. It was an uplifting experience for him. His intellectual and literary abilities were at last recognised and he came back to Calcutta in a happy frame of mind.

Soon after his return he got an offer to write and also broadcast talks on a freelance basis from the Calcutta station of the All India

Radio (AIR). The credit for this offer should go to Mother. She had become rather friendly with a family living in a flat on the first floor of Jatindra Mansion. The lady of this family persuaded her husband, Nalini Kanta Sarkar, a comic writer and also an editor of a Bengali journal published by AIR, to introduce Father to the Station Director of Calcutta. Nirad Chaudhuri now had a regular income from AIR and five years later it would be this contact that would help him to get a regular job in Delhi at the News Services Division of AIR.

However, later in July 1937, Nirad Chaudhuri received a call from Suresh Chandra Majumdar, one of the founders and owners of *Ananda Bazaar Patrika* as well as *The Hindustan Standard*. Suresh Babu asked Father to see Sarat Chandra Bose, a leading barrister of Calcutta and a front ranking leader of the Congress Party, who was also the elder brother of the charismatic leader Netaji Subhas Chandra Bose. After his release from jail in 1936, Sarat Chandra Bose had regained his stature as a lawyer and a nationalist leader. He needed an able secretary and, according to Suresh Majumdar, there was no better person in Bengal than Nirad Chaudhuri. His appointment to this position signalled the end of a significant, but extremely trying phase in Father's life. In a prefatory note included in *The Autobiography of an Unknown Indian* he wrote: 'I entered the world in 1921, and for sixteen years after that suffered such poverty, want and humiliation as I cannot wish even an enemy, if I had any, to be punished with.'

Photograph of Sarat Chandra Bose (right).
Picture courtesy Netaji Research Bureau, Calcutta.

Though Nirad Chaudhuri's creative talents as a writer suffered a period of eclipse since becoming a secretary to Sarat Bose, he gained a deep insight into the mindset of many national leaders and their political modus operandi. Working with a steady determination, fighting all odds of long hours and often unpleasant situations arising from many hangers-on surrounding the politicians, Father often came home not only exhausted, but also fuming at the double standards of behaviour that he noticed among many of the top-level leaders of the time. To escape from

Sound box of a gramophone made by E.M. Ginn, which Nirad Chaudhuri bought for two hundred rupees in 1939.

work-related stress, he took the task of educating his young sons with utmost seriousness. He would also listen to records of Western classical music even though he had to borrow a gramophone from a friend.

However, for us two brothers the end of 1937 was a time of grave crisis. One evening both Kirti and I went down with a serious attack of diphtheria. Our doctor uncle came over to the house, injected us with a serum and warned that the side-effects of that injection could be serious. According to Mother, I was practically unconscious throughout that night, which was the new year's eve of 1938; Father returned home long after midnight. He brought one of the first antibiotics, Prontocil, prescribed by my uncle. That medicine was available only at an all-night chemist shop, which was called Frank Ross, on Chowringhee. After reading the information leaflet of the new drug and finding that a protein supplement was essential, my parents saw to it that we had an egg a day for our breakfast. When we recovered from that dreaded illness, Father bought us a large Meccano set that would put us on to the path of tinkering with all things mechanical. By that time he had also made up his mind not to send us to any school and bought various books such as *Modern Teachings* and *The Practical Infant Teachers*. Mother would do most of the teaching and Father provided a general background of science and arithmetic. In the beginning, our mother tongue Bengali was taught in great detail and by the time I was six, books for children and magazines such as *Sandesh* kept me busy.

Occasionally, when Sarat Bose took a break and visited his country home in Rishra or went for a week's holiday to Kurseong, Father would have time to take us to the Alipore Zoo to show us various kinds of animals or to the Indian Museum to show us the fossils of prehistoric reptiles such as the dinosaurs. We also loved going to the Eden Gardens and seeing the Burmese Pagoda. There would be giant leaves of water lilies called Victoria Regina there for us to see. But the real excitement came one day when, along with our cousin

Krishna Didi and my eldest uncle, we went off to the temple of Dakshineswar, where Sri Ramakrishna Paramhansa had preached and lived. While we were crossing Bally or Willingdon Bridge on foot, a large seaplane of the Imperial Airways flew down the River Ganges and landed near the Bally Bridge.

Our first visit to Dumdum Airport was equally exciting. A British warplane of that era called Bristol Beaufort was refuelling at Dumdum. It was probably on its way to Rangoon or Singapore. Father, with his extensive knowledge of aviation, immediately pointed out the various parts of that twin-engine plane such as the wings, elevators and the rudder.

Given that there was now a steady inflow of income, Nirad Chaudhuri began to collect records (78 rpm only and made of fragile shellac) in spite of the fact that he did not have a gramophone of his own. Once in a while Father resorted to a little subterfuge with Mother for buying such expensive record albums. A set of such records was the *Clarinet Quintet* by Brahms. Whenever I listen to it I cannot help but remember how Mother had discovered that set hidden behind a stack of art books. After returning from work, Father found, to his chagrin, this album displayed prominently on the sitting room divan and was completely crestfallen.

Nirad Chaudhuri's three sons, Dhruva at the gramophone, Kirti (sitting) and Prithvi on the floor with their mother, 1941. Picture courtesy Sisir Chaudhuri.

Till 1939 Father had steadily refused to buy a gramophone as he could not find one that was up to his high standards. Every few weeks there would be a new catalogue from a handmade gramophone-maker called E.M. Ginn. One evening, when Kirti and I had returned home after a long weekend at our uncle's place, we saw a gramophone with a huge exponential horn rising high above our head. An English army officer from Fort William had been recalled home and he had sold his machine to Father for two hundred rupees. No serious record buff would use a steel needle those days as shellac records were fragile and needles made of either bamboo or thorn had to be sharpened after two sides were played. That, along with the winding of the clockwork motor, made the task of playing one of Beethoven's symphonies really formidable.

Checking facts about the freedom movement, Oxford, 1992.

Nirad Chaudhuri's collection of Western classical music was perhaps among the best in Calcutta. Seventy years later I still remember that many friends such as Satyajit Ray, also literary figures such as Chanchal Chatterjee, Bibhuti Bhusan Bannerji and Amal Home accompanied by an American lady called Adrianne Moor, often came to our home for recorded music recitals. There would also be an English clergyman called Ronald Ship among the listeners, who would often break out into snatches of operatic airs in his deep baritone voice. Years later, Satyajit Ray recalled in one of his autobiographies that I, as a young boy of six or seven, could recognise Haydn's *Quartet No. 1, Opus 1,* in less than a minute after the music began.

Farewell Calcutta

Whiteway & Ladlow building, a department store of the 1940s, Calcutta.

From the spring of 1939 the adults in our family, including Father and Uncle Binu, appeared to be rather excited about the outcome of the Tripuri meeting of the All India Congress Committee (AICC). That particular meeting went totally against Rashtrapati Subhas Bose, as he was known in Congress circles in those days, and even Sarat Chandra Bose was drawn into the bitter acrimony between Mahatma Gandhi and Subhas Bose. Resigning from the Congress Party after this controversy, Subhas Babu formed his own political party known till today as the Forward Bloc. This rift among senior Congress leaders as well as what had been observed at the AICC meetings in Sarat Babu's house in the autumn of 1937 brought about a fundamental change in Nirad Chaudhuri's attitude towards the Indian leaders. He became cynical towards them, the only exception being Sarat Babu, who was always held in great esteem by Father even when their views on world politics were radically different.

A few weeks before 1 September 1939, when Germany attacked Poland, Father had an argument with Subhas Bose and Sarat Babu. They could not believe that Great Britain would ever fight Hitler. As a matter of fact, it so followed that when some taunting remarks were being made about Nirad

On the banks of Bindu Saravar lake, Bhubaneswar, Orissa, where the Chaudhuris went for a holiday in 1939.

Chaudhuri's views, Nazimuddin, a Minister in the Bengal Government, rang up Sarat Babu to inform him that both Great Britain and France had declared war on Germany. Sarat Bose was generous enough to say, 'Nirad Babu, your prediction on this war has proved to be right.'

The very next morning we saw a twin-engine plane with Royal Air Force markings flying all over Calcutta; Father identified it as a Blenheim bomber. Soon that bomber was joined by a single-engine fighter plane, probably a Hawkers Hurricane. Observing what was being discussed around us, my younger brother and I began mock battles with our air guns, which had been presented to us on his birthday on 8 September 1939.

About a month later, at the time of the Durga Puja holidays, our family along with that of my eldest uncle who was a lawyer decided to visit the seaside town of Puri and the temple town of Bhubaneswar. Going for a holiday to a sea beach with our cousin Krishna Didi was a proposition that thrilled us the young boys; Father, too, was excited. His favourite niece, nicknamed Bitchhu, was always great company even when his three young sons were there. My youngest brother Prithvi Narayan had been born a few months prior to this on 20 May 1939. Father referred to this baby as his Benjamin, probably because it was the beginning of a prosperous period for our family.

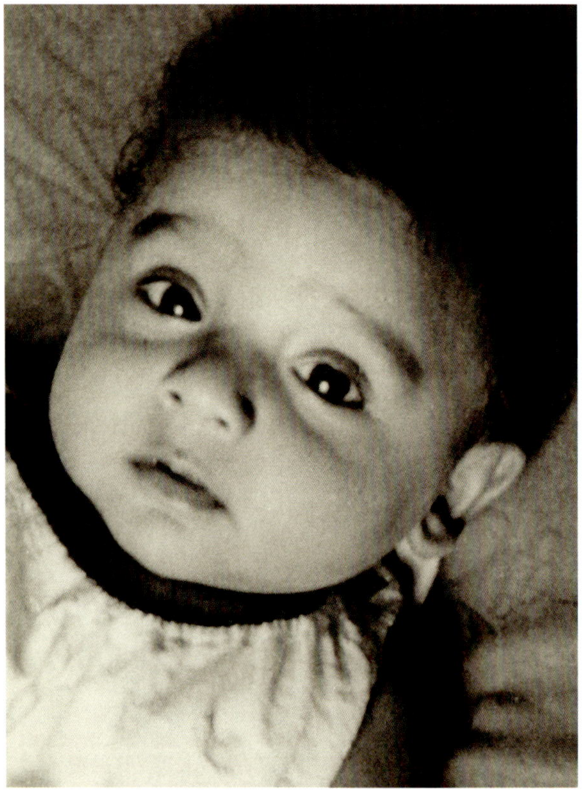

Prithvi, also called Benjamin, the youngest son of Nirad Chaudhuri.

When we were to visit Puri, Prithvi was about five months old, and there were serious misgivings among Mother's relatives about an overnight train journey with this baby. However, Uncle Binu, the most practical member in the family, bought a cane cradle and, after lining it with a cotton quilt, made the little one quite comfortable once we boarded the Puri Express. The first stop on our trip was at Bhubaneswar, now the capital city of Orissa. It was not an important station in 1939, and the Puri Express stopped there for just two minutes. All of us had to jump out quickly. But once our luggage was counted and we came out of the railway station, the temple spires gleaming in the morning sun appeared like an enchanted engraving done by one of the Daniel brothers. Soon, we reached a *dharmashala*, or a pilgrim's shelter, on the banks of the sacred lake called Bindu Sarovar.

In less than an hour after our arrival, I escaped what would have been sure death by drowning in the holy waters of that lake. Father, always eager that we should have new experiences, took Kirti and me to Bindu Sarovar. After our dip he placed us on one of the steps and began to swim into the deep waters of the lake. Suddenly, I slipped from the stone step I was sitting on and Kirti, only five at that time, failed to raise an alarm. Fortunately, Uncle Charu, who was standing nearby, jumped into the lake and rescued me from sure death.

Our next misadventure, or rather an escape from what could have been a serious problem, happened the same day. Father had insisted that we carry our air guns and dress in *khaki* uniforms. When we marched out to a solitary temple called Mukteshwar, an Anglo-Indian police officer rushed up suddenly on a bicycle and asked us to stop and hand over our guns. Luckily, the presence of mind of my

Sarat Bose's car in which Netaji Subhas Bose was driven out of Calcutta. Picture courtesy Netaji Reseach Bureau.

lawyer uncle and Nirad Chaudhuri's fluency of speech saved our sightseeing trip from turning into a disaster.

Next morning we went to visit the caves of Udaygiri and Khandagiri. This was to be our first ride in a bullock cart. Father's original idea of starting at dawn was shot down by his elder brother when he heard from some cart drivers that tigers or leopards were often sighted near those caves and herds of elephants at times blocked the road in search of their favourite delicacies such as sugarcane or rice. When I told this story to my wife and daughter, while visiting Puri and Bhubaneswar in 1986, they could hardly believe me.

After two more days of touring temples such as the Lingaraja and Ananta Vasudeva, we began our journey to Puri. What intrigued us as children was the sight of a *pankha* or a hand-pulled fan inside the upper-class waiting-room at the railway station. From

Remembering his days in Sarat Bose's house in Calcutta, and his move to Delhi, for a television film, 1970.

the Khurda Road Junction, when the passenger train turned east towards Puri, Father insisted that we should repeat the names of every station such as Sakshi Gopal and Malatipatpur. This was an obsession that Nirad Chaudhuri could never resist and he took great delight in showing off the precocious knowledge of his boys. Later, as the temple of Lord Jagannath appeared across the swampy plain next to the railway line, Father became eloquent once again, narrating his first impression of the famous temple. Apparently, Father had visited Puri in 1926 with his sister Priyabala and her husband to escape the drudgery and frustration of clerical work at the Military Accounts Department in Calcutta.

Hornby model train, gifted to Dhruva Chaudhuri by his father.

Our holiday in Puri raised the spirits of everyone except my eldest aunt. She fractured her ankle while trying to swim across a large wave of surf. I, who was prone to misadventure, had no other mishap, except getting a hard blow on my back from Kirti, while fighting a mock battle with our air guns. As a punishment, Father did not allow my brother to eat his lunch that afternoon. But, our eldest uncle took pity on the little boy and asked him to share the lunch from his own large *thali* (plate). Nirad Chaudhuri could not contradict the wishes of his eldest brother and so Kirti dug into all the delicacies, including prawn curry and pieces of fried fish. It may be interesting to note that, even in a non-joint family such as ours, the authority of an elder brother was always held supreme.

We returned to Calcutta after the plaster cast around my aunt's ankle was removed. But soon after we came back Mother had a severe attack of pleurisy and was laid up for the whole of that winter till the spring of 1940. Father engaged a nurse to look after her and Prithvi. Since Mother was advised to take complete bed rest, we had problems with our studies. Fortunately, Uncle Binu introduced a fellow freedom fighter, K.K. Biswas, to Father and he was to become our private tutor for over two years from that point onwards.

During Christmas that year Father took us to Whiteway & Ladlow. The entire first floor was reserved for toys and for the first time we saw more than one Hornby model train running all over the shop floor. Father promised to buy us a train soon after Mother got well. He got the latest catalogue of Hornby trains and would spend long hours in drawing various combinations of track layout. Incidentally, a model train for me came as late as 1965; it was the reward for illustrating an important article on India by Father, published by *The Times of London*.

Nirad Chaudhuri became really busy with his war commentaries for AIR. He also began to write regularly on World War II for a business magazine called *The Capital*, which was edited by an Englishman called Sir Geoffrey Tyson. It was, of course, no surprise that Sarat Bose received many complaints about Nirad Chaudhuri's pro-British writings and even about his loyalty towards a prominent Congress leader. It was extremely generous of Father's employer to brush off those complaints by saying that Nirad Babu was entitled to have his own political views and opinions, and free to express them in his broadcasts as well as writings. Not only that, Sarat Bose even suggested that our family should move into his son-in-law's house, which was lying vacant in the nearby locality of Bhawanipur.

In September 1940, as the German air force was extensively bombing many cities of England and had brought several countries of Europe under its occupation, we moved into an old but spacious two-storeyed house, which was less than a ten minute walk from Father's workplace, which was No. 1, Woodburn Park. The house we moved into had eight fair-sized rooms and two wide corridors. There was also a paved courtyard and a narrow garden alongside the main building. Kirti and I really ran amuck on getting so much space to play in and we expanded our activities from flying model aeroplanes to playing regular football matches with the neighbouring children.

But at the beginning of 1941, Mother became ill once again with a serious chest infection and was confined to her bedroom. To make matters worse, one of my unemployed uncles, along with his eldest son Chinmoy, was compelled to move into a ground floor room, which was earlier occupied by a revolutionary leader, Tridib Chaudhuri. Tridib Kaka (Uncle), as we called him, was one of Father's friends. He was arrested one morning from our house, where Father had sublet a room to him to offset the steep rise in rents. Tridib Chaudhuri was to go on to become a Member of the Indian Parliament.

After moving into our new house on Chakraberia Road, we began to visit Woodburn Park quite often to play with Sarat Babu's children, Subrata and Chitra. On some of our visits we also saw their elder brother, Dr Sisir Kumar Bose, who shortly afterwards was to drive Netaji Subhas Bose to Dhanbad in Bihar, and then help him escape to Germany via Kabul. At that point in time no outsider in Calcutta, or even in India, would have been able to guess where Subhas Bose had suddenly disappeared. My father, however, in spite of receiving a note from Subhas Bose about certain correspondence with Mahatma Gandhi on the very day Bose left Calcutta, believed that even Sarat Bose did not know the exact destination of his famous brother.

On 7 December 1941, as is well known, Japan attacked Pearl Harbour and practically destroyed the entire American navy and air force stationed in Hawaii. The Japanese planes also sank two British battleships—the Prince of Wales and Repulse—at the Singapore Harbour. This news came as a big shock for everyone and frantic preparations began in Calcutta for possible air attacks by Japanese bombers. All parks and playgrounds, including the Northern Park nearest to our house, were dug up and trenches made as a precaution against air raids. Even in some of the private houses of Calcutta spare ground floor rooms were reinforced with sand bags and heavy shutters to serve as improvised air raid shelters.

Five days later, Sarat Bose was arrested from his own house. Kirti and I were playing in the garden with his children, when all of a sudden our playmates were called in by their mother Bibha Bose. My brother and I rushed home unescorted and told Mother that something serious had happened at Woodburn Park. Within minutes Uncle Binu arrived with Amal Home, who confirmed the news of the arrest. Nirad Chaudhuri lost his well-paid job for no fault of his. My parents were hit once again by difficult times, but Father continued with his regular broadcasts at the Calcutta station of AIR and also carried on writing for *The Bengal Weekly* and *The Capital*.

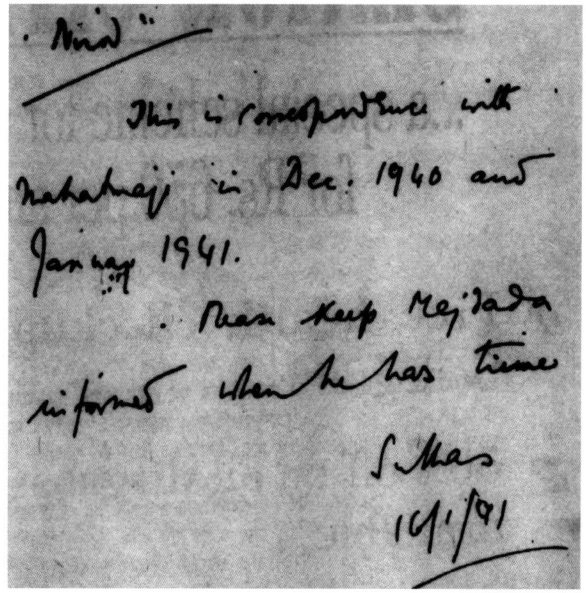
Nirad

This is correspondence with Mahatmaji in Dec. 1940 and January 1941.

Please keep Mejdada informed when he has time

Subhas
16/1/41

A note written by Netaji Subhas Bose to Nirad Chaudhuri on the day the former disappeared from Calcutta. Courtesy Netaji Research Bureau.

The marriage of Father's fifth brother, Manmatha Chaudhuri, took place at this crucial juncture. This uncle of ours was an electrical engineer and was working at the Tata Steel plant in Jamshedpur. He rarely came to Calcutta and for us youngsters it was indeed a wonderful occasion to make merry, even though there were threats of Japanese air attacks on Calcutta. This was also the time when the entire Chaudhuri family, adults and children, would have a group photograph taken, with the exception of Father's two sisters who were living in East Bengal at that time and could not attend the wedding because of heavy troop movement.

Nirad Chaudhuri (extreme right, last row) with his brothers and their families on the occasion of Manmatha's wedding.

We pulled along because of the many wartime broadcasts done by Father. But, one afternoon, he came back from the radio station looking quite upset and told Mother that there had been a strong exchange of words with the Controller, Ahmed Shah Bokhari. This gentleman had taken Nirad Chaudhuri to task because of a note, which he had given to Tyson regarding the war broadcast policy of AIR. However, after a week, there was a telephone call from Bokhari, who offered Father a job at AIR for Rs 250 per month. That offer was straightaway refused because of the meagre amount; Bokhari said that he would think over the matter. After a gap of a week or ten days there was an offer once again from Bokhari. It was for a job in Delhi at a salary of Rs 400 and this time there was no question of refusing. For quite some time Mother had been saying that there was no future for Nirad Chaudhuri in Calcutta and her own health had continued to be indifferent so a change in air would help.

And So to Delhi

P&O Building on Delhi's Nicholson Road, where Nirad Chaudhuri lived with his family for twenty-eight years.

Moving to Delhi in March 1942 was in a sense to prove to be even more significant for Nirad Chaudhuri than settling in Oxford. He was to take up a job outside Calcutta for the first time and also wear European clothes. Before this Father had once attended a news conference called by Lord Wavell, then Commander-in-Chief of India, but he had dressed in a *dhoti* and kurta. Now, he got a tropical suit made along with a couple of shirts. As for the knotting of a tie, Mother had a hard time teaching Father to do that, and a measure of satisfaction was reached only a few hours before the Toofan Express to Delhi that he was taking moved out of Howrah Station.

Unfortunately, my maternal grandmother died on the same night that Nirad Chaudhuri left for Delhi. My grandparents had moved to a remote town called Behrampur due to the threat of Japanese air attacks. Though Father was totally against such evacuation by any of our relatives, it seemed my grandmother was relieved to know before her death that Nirad and his family would move on to Delhi, far from the range of Japanese bombers and a possible naval invasion, too. We reached Behrampur a day after Uncle Binu had received the sad news while he was in his office. It was really difficult for Mother who was very close to her parents, but there was hardly any time for her to grieve and we returned to Calcutta within three days to prepare for our journey to Delhi and to wind up the establishment in Calcutta.

It was the last week of March 1942 when Mother received a letter from Father saying that a reasonable accommodation had been fixed near the Mori Gate area of Old Delhi and she, along with us the three brothers, accompanied by our tutor K.K. Biswas and attendant Dhanukdhari, should start for Delhi as soon as possible. The difficulty lay in arranging money for the journey. Since there was no surplus cash, Father wrote that Mother should try to get the money that was due to him from a few articles and features that had been published in some newspapers

The Kodak box camera, which was presented by Nirad Chaudhuri to his sons in 1941.

and magazines. But in the end Mother had to start the journey all the way to Delhi with Rs 100 borrowed from her two brothers-in-law.

That journey by a third-class coach was really tough. There was also the scare of Japanese bombing, along with the heat and dust of the North Indian plains. It was no exaggeration when I wrote in my book *Delhi: Light, Shades, Shadows*, that our journey to Delhi was somewhat similar to Boris Pasternak's description of the train journey to Siberia in *Dr Zhivago*. This journey, with its ups and downs, took around twenty-four hours. At the end of which, having passed the gleaming pavilions of the Red Fort, which Father had found disappointing on his first journey here, our train moved into the Old Delhi Station. Father, impeccably dressed in a suit, complete with a tie and a felt hat on his head, rushed towards an upper-class coach. When he found that his family had travelled in a plebian third-class coach, he snatched our baby brother from Mother's arms and stood haughtily aloof. The handling of his precious possessions, such as the gramophone with a large horn, heavy records and the full-sized reproduction of Mona Lisa, was left to Mother and K.K. Biswas.

On reaching our residence, P&O Building on Nicholson Road, my younger brother and I were hugely excited to see the old wall of Shahjahanbad and also a distant stone gate called Kashmiri Darwaza. The lush greenery of Civil Lines along with that of the Ridge, visible from our flat, created a sense of wonder in us. For Father, too, this flat was to be a big relief and escape from the dreary hutments and mosquitoes of Timarpur where he had been living so far.

For the first fortnight in Delhi, Father had stayed with Rajen Sen, a colleague and also once the halfback of the famous Mohan Bagan football team. Though this gentleman and his family members spared no pains to make Nirad Chaudhuri comfortable, he found the hot Bengali cooking along with the dry privies of Timarpur rather difficult to accept. Only the nearness of the Ridge, along with the River Yamuna flowing near Metcalfe House, provided some sort of a relief. So he wasted no time in renting a flat on Nicholson Road and rather than moving in alone urged Mother to join him soon with their three sons.

After spending the first night at Timarpur, Father would have been inclined to rush back to Calcutta had it not been for his English superior, Charles Barnes, who proved to be rather congenial. Fortunately, due to Barnes and also the fact that our new flat was within walking distance of his office, his spirits soon rose. As it was to turn out, he would continue to live in Delhi for the next twenty-eight years and that, too, in the same flat. This was one of the longest periods of his uninterrupted stay in a place except the twenty-nine years he spent in Oxford. It was

The All India Radio News Services Division group; Nirad Chaudhuri is seated third from the left in the second row and Charles Barnes is third from the right.

also to be in Delhi that Nirad Chaudhuri would finally establish himself as an author of great international repute.

In a typical bent of mind that was characteristic of Nirad Chaudhuri, he wrote to Mother saying that our stay in Delhi might only be for only six months. This, however, did not prevent her from bringing all the necessary household items including all the utensils and a Primus stove ready with some kerosene. So from the very first night of our arrival, Father had the luxury of having a home-cooked meal of rice and lentils, accompanied by boiled potatoes and eggs. By next morning Mother had arranged for the charcoal required for cooking and some fresh food stuff such as milk and vegetables; even fish available from local vendors had been bought.

On most days, Nirad Chaudhuri would go for his walks early in the morning and on his return would tell us about the old monuments or new sights he had seen. His office hours usually started at 3 pm and he would return home after his evening broadcast scheduled at 8.50 pm. Both the office and studios of AIR were not far from Mori Gate. Father would usually walk that distance of about a mile, except during very hot afternoons. On such occasions he would hire a *tonga* and I remember Mother giving him about six *annas* for his fare. No matter what the outside temperature was, Father wore a tropical suit, along with a tie and felt hat, which was changed to a *sola topi* during the hottest days of summer. One afternoon, when it was cool after a sudden dust storm, Father asked Kirti and I to walk to his office on Alipur Road, now Shyam Nath Marg.

The first photograph of Nirad Chaudhuri taken by Dhruva in 1946. A box camera shot reproduced from a newspaper article.

Nirad Chaudhuri's wartime duties were mostly in the afternoons or evenings, but he would usually remain busy in the morning studying various war fronts from detailed maps, which were especially provided for writing his war commentaries. Within a few weeks of our coming to Delhi, Sir Stafford Cripps, a cabinet minister from England, had flown in with an offer of granting a Dominion Status to India in lieu of cooperation by nationalist leaders in World War II. However, this offer was summarily rejected by all Congress leaders including Mahatma Gandhi. One evening after the failure of his mission, Father saw Sir Stafford Cripps entering one of the studios of AIR to make a broadcast and he recounted how he was struck by the pleasant and amiable expression on the British politician's face in spite of the political rebuff he had just received.

It was generally left to K.K. Biswas to take us to places such as Chandni Chowk or Kashmere Gate and sometimes even to

In a suit stitched by Phelps & Co, Connaught Place, New Delhi, 1948.

Connaught Place. I still remember having my first glass of cold coffee at India Coffee House, which had opened its first branch at Chandni Chowk next to the well-known pharmacy of Dr H.C. Sen. Father was not happy to hear that we had drunk coffee and warned us against it in no uncertain terms. But in less than a year's time he himself had got addicted to hot coffee, taken especially while visiting the library of the Imperial Archives, now renamed National Archives, on Queen's Way or Janpath. In those days, Father would sometimes walk up to the library to study the history of Islamic culture and architecture.

In the summer of 1943 we saw our first film in Delhi at the Odeon cinema-house in Connaught Place. The film chosen by Father was a full-length documentary called *The Desert Victory* and it was based on the actual war footage taken at the battle of El Alamein in Egypt. Later, we also saw the caravan of General Von Arnheim, the defeated German general, exhibited in front of the Regal Theatre in Connaught Circus. On such occasions we would usually walk all the way from the Old City to New Delhi.

Shortly after Father's office shifted to the new Broadcasting House in New Delhi he began to change his food habits from rice, lentils and fish to *roti*, vegetables and mutton curry. Perhaps it was the acute shortage of rice that followed the Bengal famine of 1943 that was responsible for this change. I have a vague feeling that this preference for eating meat and a North Indian diet began after he read about the food habits of the Muslim rulers of India.

In the summer of 1944 Nirad Chaudhuri became the Talks Officer at the News Services Division of AIR. I clearly remember that he had attended that interview dressed in a beige three-piece tropical suit with a maroon tie. This outfit, including a stiff-collared shirt, was especially stitched by the English outfitters, Phelps & Co of A Block, Connaught Place. Many of Father's journalist colleagues from Calcutta, also called for the same interview, were amazed to see the change in his appearance. But there were serious problems before the appointment order could be formalised. Though Father had no indication of this trouble, the Criminal Investigation Department (CID) of Calcutta police raised serious objections about his job with Sarat Bose and also his nationalist activities of the thirties. Charles Barnes, Bokhari and Sir Frederic Puckle, Secretary, Information and Broadcasting, overruled those objections. However, Barnes, as his immediate chief, asked Father to keep away from people with nationalist tendencies. These included Lala Shankar Lal, who met Father one night with a secret letter from Sarat Babu, who at the time was in Coonoor jail in the Nilgiri Hills.

Sanat and Prithvi with Rex who was from the Maharaja of Jind's kennel.

Father would now have no less than four new colleagues who were supposed to have assisted him. But, assistants or not, Nirad Chaudhuri's workload increased considerably till Germany surrendered to the Allied Forces in May 1945. Father was greatly disturbed by the sudden death of US President Roosevelt and the defeat of Prime Minister Churchill in the polls. After taking a few days leave to recover, he started writing articles on British politics and taking us out for long walks accompanied by our new dog Rex, who had arrived from the kennel of the Maharaja of Jind. Father also encouraged us to go on birdwatching trips along with him; the gift of a pair of old binoculars from an English colonel had made that activity really interesting. Apart from the Ridge and the River Yamuna, our walks took us to Roshanara Bagh and even up to Lodi Garden and the Humayun's Tomb. The view, from the roof of that building, of the river and its east bank stretching up to the horizon, was spectacular at the time.

The family at the P&O Building, a box camera shot, Delhi, 1948.

Shortly afterwards, we got an opportunity to get to know an aristocratic Muslim family really well. Among his four colleagues in the Talks Unit, Nirad Chaudhuri had one elderly journalist, Sayyad Mahmood Rizvi, who apart from being a lawyer and journalist was an eminent Urdu poet and knew the Persian script well. He helped Father to decipher many of the Persian inscriptions found on the historic buildings of Delhi. This inspired Nirad Chaudhuri to plan a book on the history of the late Mughal period, particularly what happened in and around the Red Fort. But soon after collecting many books about that period and subject, he seemed to have lost the initiative. Around the same time he began to follow a new interest—buying Mason, Spode and Paragon chinaware and cut-glass pieces from the Sutherland's showroom on Janpath!

Nirad Chaudhuri's dining table, he always believed in entertaining lavishly.

Along with buying these items, which he could ill afford, Father began to throw grand parties and serve vintage wine with European culinary treats prepared at home. During those parties I had to bear the brunt of buying exotic fruits and flowers such as strawberries and narcissi from Connaught Place, and polishing the wafer-thin wine glasses to serve a 1934 Veuve Clicquot champagne at an exact temperature specified by Father. This feat was not easy in a household without a refrigerator!

As the level of entertaining guests went up to a crescendo, Father also began to receive return invitations to attend various parties at Chelmsford Club, Imperial Hotel and at the nearby Cecil Hotel in Civil Lines. While his English guests wore tuxedos, Father immediately got a formal evening dress made, complete with a tailcoat and white waistcoat, at an English establishment called Ranken & Co. The Calcutta killings in August 1946, however, greatly disturbed Nirad Chaudhuri. He only felt somewhat better after three of his articles on politics in Britain were published in a magazine called *New English Review*. Then, at the invitation of his colleague Rizvi Sahib, all of us went to Agra. We got to see the Taj Mahal for the first time, visited Sikandra and spent a whole day at Fatehpur Sikri. I remember Father saying that more than the Taj, how impressed he was by Fatehpur Sikri.

That week in Agra with Rizvi Sahib's family at his *haveli* (mansion) was a wonderful time for us. It was a long cherished holiday for Nirad Chaudhuri, the first after coming

With his family at Taj Mahal, Agra, 1946. His colleague Sayyad Mahmood Rizvi's son, Hassan, is on the left.

to Delhi. He had at last got to see some of the finest examples of Mughal architecture with his own eyes. In the second part of his autobiography, *Thy Hand, Great Anarch!*, he mentions that one of the gains of coming to Delhi was adding to his knowledge of Islamic history and seeing many of the best examples of Muslim architecture.

An Unknown Indian

Nirad Chaudhuri writing The Autobiography of an Unknown Indian *on his Underwood typewriter, August 1947. Photograph by Krishna Bose, taken with a box camera.*

When Father got married in April 1932, he had been presented with a small but sturdy secretariat table. Immediately after that he had acquired a portable typewriter made by a company called Underwood. That machine was actually ordered for his elder brother, who was an advocate. But at the last moment he had second thoughts about it and so Father decided to take it. For ten long years, however, that gaunt little machine would be more or less a decorative piece on Father's writing table and only after it would be brought to Delhi, packed in a bedroll, that it would be put to use.

From 1945 onwards Nirad Chaudhuri would occasionally type out a letter or an article for the British Press and at times even a script for one of his AIR broadcasts. I was given the responsibility of posting those letters or articles at the General Post Office near Kashmere Gate and also walking or cycling to the Broadcasting House in Parliament Street. At times the weather in Delhi used to be quite hostile, but nothing mattered to Father except the fact that all his writings should reach their destination at the stipulated time.

One hot morning in May 1947, we the brothers and our cousin Sanat, who had come to visit us from East Bengal, saw Father typing away without a break. He had not even asked for his usual morning coffee. The little Underwood machine was propped up on a wooden stool and Father sat on a reed seat called a *moorah*. We had no inkling about what was being typed. Sanat got a fierce growl when he tried to catch a glimpse of what Father was writing. At first we thought that Father was excited about some ongoing political happening in India and wanted to give vent to his feelings. Soon after finishing a couple of pages, Nirad Chaudhuri got up and announced that he had started a book on his own life beginning from Kishorganj. Fifty years later, he mentioned in a television interview that he could not sleep for several nights and thought that his death was imminent after the age of fifty. In the same interview Father went on to say that instead of writing a formal and scholarly book on a historical topic as he had thought of earlier, he decided to write about his own life, as seen from a historical point of view. Within a few days he had finalised the name of the book—*The Autobiography of an Unknown Indian*. From then on there was no break, not even for a single day. Right from about 4.30 in the morning, Nirad Chaudhuri would sit

Facing page: The Underwood typewriter, bought in 1932, was used to write several books and about fifty articles.

The final proof of The Autobiography of an Unknown Indian*, 1951.*

down at his typewriter and turn out at least four or five pages before having breakfast at 9. Regular office hours were hardly a matter of concern then. The maximum time that Father would spend at AIR was from 10 in the morning to 1 in the afternoon. Fortunately for him the Director, Mehra Masani, realised the great potential Father had as a writer and so, along with the

Nirad Chaudhuri enjoying a cup of coffee with his wife at home, Delhi, 1947.

Director-General, Colonel Laxmanan, did not insist on a 10-to-5 attendance.

Though Mother was somewhat distraught at these unusual office hours that Father followed, she kept her composure and managed all the household affairs, including the finance and entertaining of guests. The three of us and our cousin were left to our own devices. Except for reading books in English ranging from Jim Corbett to Sir Walter Scott, and at times even turning over the pages of Romain Rolland's *Jean Christoff*, we had no formal education at that time. But that did not seem to bother Nirad Chaudhuri; he was sure that once his book was complete, all the shortcomings in our formal education would be made up. On 3 June 1947 came the news that India would be partitioned. I still remember the fury with which Father

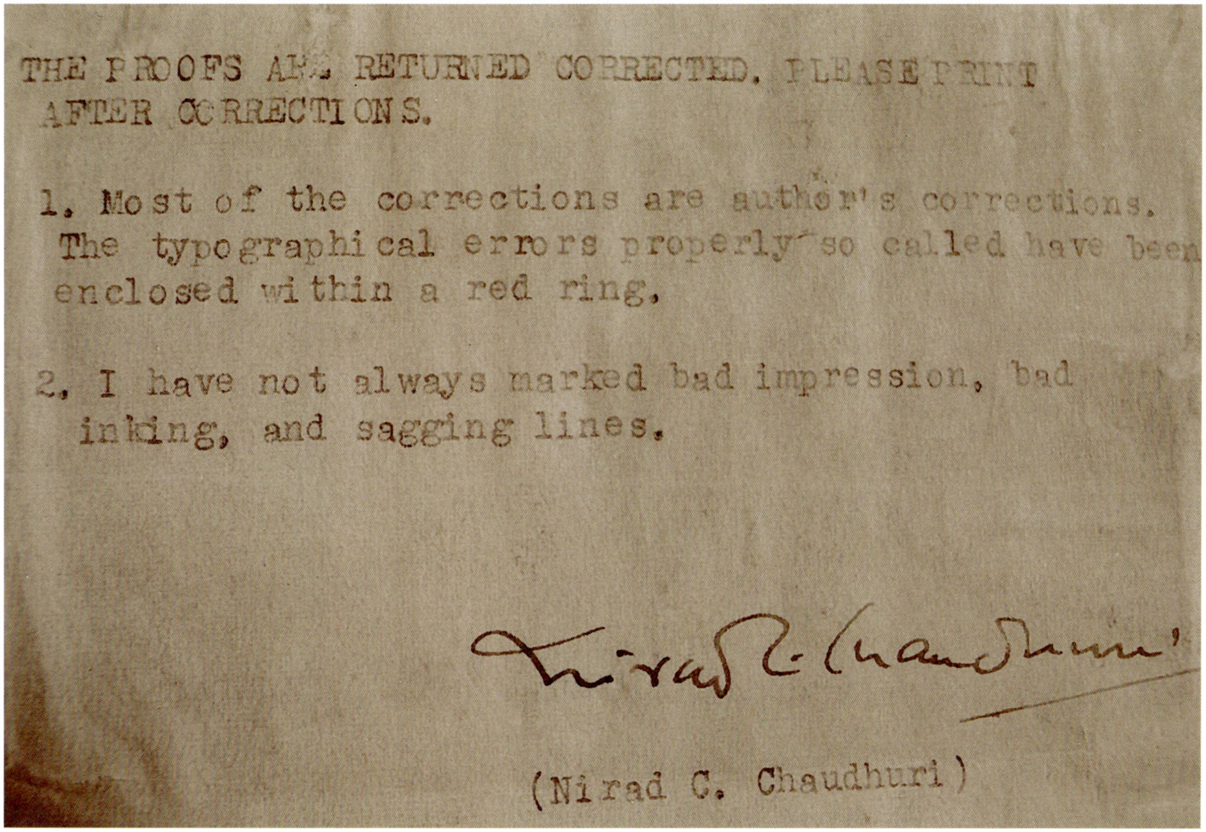

THE PROOFS ARE RETURNED CORRECTED. PLEASE PRINT AFTER CORRECTIONS.

1. Most of the corrections are author's corrections. The typographical errors properly so called have been enclosed within a red ring.

2. I have not always marked bad impression, bad inking, and sagging lines.

Nirad C. Chaudhuri

(Nirad C. Chaudhuri)

Approved proof of The Autobiography of an Unknown Indian, *giving a go-ahead for printing the famous book.*

threw away the newspaper and shouted that Partition would bring more trouble than peace. When the long-awaited Independence Day came on 15 August 1947, we boys along with our cousin Krishna Didi, who was spending her holidays with us, had to use a great deal of persuasion to get permission to hear Pandit Nehru's speech, 'India's Tryst with Destiny' and also witness the historic celebrations near Parliament House. The flypast by a group of Spitfire fighters was my first attempt at capturing a historic event with a camera.

In less than a fortnight, Nirad Chaudhuri's prophecy that there would be more trouble than peace after Partition started proving to be true. From the last week of August, serious incidents of violence and rioting started breaking out all over Delhi, including in Connaught Place. On that morning, when Pandit Nehru tried to prevent the looting of some New Delhi shops using a police

Left to right: The three Chaudhuri brothers, Kirti, Prithvi and Dhruva, at their residence in Delhi.

lathi (stick), Father was on his way to the Broadcasting House on a cycle. He returned home in the office transport escorted by two policemen armed with 303 rifles. He was completely shattered and for the rest of the day went on talking to himself about the consequences of partition.

For the next fortnight or so there was chaos all over the city. The visual and aural indications of arson and rioting were obvious to us even when confined to our houses. Father would often refuse to believe the news of gun battles or the looting of shops that went on near Mori Gate. If I reported what I had seen or heard from our rooftop, he would flare up and scold me for spreading stories about a canard. But, more often than not, radio announcements, or the newspaper reports the next day, confirmed what I had said and Father's impression of everything being under control would prove totally wrong.

Nirad Chaudhuri had an intense aversion for electric fans and radio receivers. No matter how hot our top floor flat at P&O Building was, Father would never allow a fan in his house. It made our lives really uncomfortable, particularly at night. And as for the radio, Father would mention specifications such as the band-spread and a push-pull output; radios with such high specifications were both expensive as well as difficult to get in the post-war market. To get over this lack of a radio-set in our house and to avoid hanging on to our landlady Mrs Pinto's modest receiver, I devised a crystal headphone receiver from war-surplus components, which I bought from the sprawling junk shops near Jama Masjid. It was with this primitive radio that I was to first hear the news of Mahatma Gandhi's assassination. Soon after I would give the news to my parents, Father would rush in, snatch my headset and start listening to the news himself.

An interesting turn of events happened in our family around this time. One morning, my two younger brothers fought over the playing rights of a toy *sarangi* (violin) sold by a street vendor and in the process the fragile musical instrument got smashed. In the pandemonium that ensued, Father promised a real violin to my youngest brother and walked out of the house. A few hours later he returned with a real half-size violin under his arm and subsequently arranged for music lessons for Prithvi from an elderly violinist, Noel Barton Jones. Soon Kirti learnt to play the piano and I learnt the viola. Supervising this trio ensemble of his three sons became the chief relaxation for Nirad Chaudhuri. It was during that rather 'musical period' that we got the opportunity to meet Pandit Ravi Shankar and his Guru, Ustad Allauddin Khan, at the studios of AIR.

Then one day we heard that Melville de Mellow, the famous newsreader of AIR, was going to England for training. Everyone was much impressed by his live coverage of Gandhiji's funeral, including the representatives of the BBC. We knew Melville de Mellow well for he had presented us with a couple of cats a few months earlier. He offered to take the half-finished manuscript of Father's autobiography to London and to give it to a publisher called Hamish Hamilton. Though this publisher showed a lot of interest at first, they later backed out after seeing the final copy because of its length as well as for certain controversial political views. It took Nirad Chaudhuri two more years and the intervention of a literary agent, before his first book, *The Autobiography of an Unknown Indian*, was accepted by the well-known publishers Macmillan & Co.

It was around this time that we were faced with two problems in our family. In July 1949, my brothers and I had gone to Calcutta for a short visit and on our return found that Father had been seriously ill. Apparently, he had fainted in his office room around lunch time and his two colleagues, Mrs Mahajan and

S.C. Bhat, had to rush him to Irwin Hospital. The symptoms were the same as that of a heart attack but the doctors were not sure. For Mother, as well as for me, that was a time for a lot of mental anxiety and financial difficulties. It would only be in the mid-1950s that Father's health would start improving. It was also at that very time that Kirti had a serious attack of typhoid. It seemed to us that he had picked up the infection while learning to swim in the River Yamuna. The only drug against typhoid, Chloromycetin, had just come into the Indian market, but doctors were not sure of its side-effects. It took Kirti more than three months to recover.

One positive reaction that these two serious crises had on our family was that Father became serious about our formal education and began to teach us regularly. He also engaged private tutors for subjects such as mathematics and science for me and a Brahman *pandit* to teach Sanskrit to Kirti. It was really tough to cover the entire syllabus of the final high school examination in just over a year. Fortunately, both Kirti and I did well as private candidates. In fact, Kirti, who got a distinction in all the arts subjects, was selected for a merit scholarship. Another experiment by our Father, fraught with very serious consequences, had proved successful and we joined Hindu College without attending a single day at any school.

When *The Autobiography of an Unknown Indian* was finally published on 8 September 1951, also Kirti's birthday, there was a great sense of jubilation in our house. Many friends and colleagues were invited for high tea; vintage champagne was later served to celebrate the twin successes of Father's book as well as my school results. Within less than a week Nirad Chaudhuri's daily post was deluged with rave reviews. The reviews by Harold Nicholson in *The Observer* and Raymond Mortimer in *The Sunday Telegraph* were the first to set the trend of serious, yet effusive reviews of *The Autobiography*. All important newspapers and journals of the British press reviewed the book. What pleased Father the most was a full-page review by Sir John Squire in *The Illustrated London News*. That page also carried a large portrait of Nirad Chaudhuri, which was taken by me specially for the article. I was duly given my first byline. According to Father, the only other Indian who had a portrait in *The Illustrated London News* till then was Pandit Nehru; that photograph was taken by the world famous portrait photographer Yousuf Karsh of Ottawa. So it was like a double celebration for our family. Then, within a matter of a few weeks, *The Autobiography of an Unknown Indian* received extensive coverage from the BBC, including the prestigious 'Third Programme' as also the World Service.

Facing page: A portrait of Nirad Chaudhuri, which effectively captures his intense expression, 1948.

Various editions of The Autobiography of An Unknown Indian.

However, the response was mostly negative from Indian newspapers and journals. One of the rare reviews on a positive note appeared in *The Statesman*, written by Dr Verrier Elwin, the well-known anthropologist. Many of Nirad Chaudhuri's Bengali friends sat on the fence when it came to the book but their ill feelings were soon found out and they had no further admittance into our flat!

The tirade of complaints by many influential people, including Krishna Menon, the then Indian High Commissioner in London, made even Prime Minister Nehru write an adverse note about Nirad Chaudhuri to the Secretary, Ministry of Information and Broadcasting. There were all kinds of questions raised about Father's income from his writings, as well as for taking the permission before one's written work is published. Finally, with no pension or gratuity sanctioned, Nirad Chaudhuri was asked to retire on 23 November 1952, his fifty-fifth birthday. It was difficult for him to get even his provident fund of Rs 3,000 or Rs 4,000 released. After nearly three months of waiting, Mother had to practically go on a *dharna*, or non-violent protest, at the room of a senior officer of the Accountant-General's office, for this negligible lifetime's savings. At that crucial time I had just joined the Delhi University as a B.Sc. Honours student and had to earn my way through college as a freelance photojournalist. V.S. Naipaul called this unusual autobiography a stupendous achievement and predicted, 'It may be the one great book to come out of the Anglo-Indian encounter.' After writing a single epoch-making book at the age of fifty, Nirad C. Chaudhuri became not only a well-known name among all Indian authors writing in English, but also a phenomenon with his knowledge of world affairs and power of writing in English.

However, Father was once again without any source of regular income. The little prosperity that he had enjoyed since 1937 came to an end. It was only after his new-found friend, Count Stanislas Ostrorog, the French Ambassador, asked Nirad Chaudhuri to look after the bulletin *News from France* that our family could carry on with the day-to-day expenses with some ease. At this crucial juncture Father was also invited to write for *The Statesman* and *The Illustrated Weekly of India*.

Author Extraordinary

The portrait of Nirad Chaudhuri reproduced in Illustrated London News *in 1951.*

For fifteen long years after 1952, give or take a few months, Nirad Chaudhuri had to fight a relentless battle not only for earning his livelihood, but also for completing two of his most successful books. *The Passage to England*, written after his first trip to England in 1955, went on to become a bestseller in England, but got mostly hostile reviews in India. Father's third book, *The Continent of Circe*, published in 1965, became the winner of the prestigious Duff Cooper Memorial Literary Prize in 1967. By then Father was also considered a leading, but critical commentator on socio-political affairs both in India and abroad.

Following the trend of the ban on his writings, most newspapers and periodicals with staunch nationalist tendencies as a rule avoided approaching Father for any of his writings. *The Statesman*, with its English editors and *The Illustrated Weekly of India* were the two notable exceptions to this informal ban. They continued to publish topical features written by Nirad Chaudhuri. Though the honorariums paid by these periodicals were good, they were hardly adequate to support our family of five, with the two elder brothers yet to complete their college education and the youngest still at school.

The only redeeming factor at that crucial time was the money that came in from the French Embassy every month and my efforts to supplement that amount by working as a part-time photojournalist. But to do that while studying was far from easy and also irregular. Prithvi took to repairing radio-sets in the neighbourhood in order to earn some pocket money. As for Kirti, a topper in many subjects, particularly history, he was not permitted to join the B.A. Honours course in Delhi University. Father insisted that Kirti be sent to England for his further studies and

A 1959 publicity campaign for A Passage to England, *which got rave reviews in England.*

yet at that time no one knew from where the money would be raised for that venture. Kirti had to wait for more than two years before he could continue with his studies at the University of London. His brilliant results there, however, made up for all the time lost.

In February 1953, after getting some unexpected money for a write-up in a foreign magazine, Father decided to visit Agra and Fatehpur Sikri. Two of his English friends, Reverend James Stuart from the Cambridge Brotherhood and John Finch, the representative of the Society for Promoting Christian Knowledge (SPCK) in Delhi went with him. Since the purpose was to write an illustrated book on Agra and Fatehpur Sikri, I had to accompany the group and take the photographs that Father desired for his proposed book. After spending a lot of time at the Taj Mahal and Agra Fort, going over the different aspects in great detail, we moved on to Fatehpur Sikri. We stayed at the old Archaeological Survey dak-bungalow for three days. That visit was unique in more ways than one, my photographs turned out well, but the book in Nirad Chaudhuri's mind never took on a concrete shape. It is unfortunate that Father's radical, yet deeply erudite, views on the architecture of Agra and Sikri remained only verbal.

Nirad Chaudhuri at Agra, with Reverend James Stuart, John Finch and Dhruva Chaudhuri.

Soon after returning from Agra there was an urgent letter from A.S. Raman, who at that time had taken over as the new editor of *The Illustrated Weekly of India* published from Bombay (now Mumbai). Father had reservations about Raman as an art critic in Delhi and his opinion about *The Illustrated Weekly* as a magazine was decidedly low. But what made Father revise his views and agree to write for the magazine was the subject, 'After Nehru Who?' Along with the request for this thought-provoking article, Raman asked Father to review some newly-published books on India and Indian politics. These offers had a profound influence on Father and turned him into a foremost writer of socio-political affairs in India with a radical view.

JUDAISM
VICTORIAN YEARS
RIVER PLATE
THE WAR FOR WORLD POWER
IF GERMANY ATTACKS

The article, 'After Nehru Who?', was published on 10 May 1953 and, as expected, elicited a strong reaction from many quarters. At the end of this article, Nirad Chaudhuri concluded that the question 'After Nehru What?' was of much greater significance for India than 'After Nehru Who?' Later in the same magazine, in its Reader's Forum, Father put forward an equally significant and topical question, 'Have We Forgotten the Mahatma?'

Knowing the financial difficulties of our family, the editor of *The Illustrated Weekly* began to send packages of newly-published books on India for review. Among them was a short novel by E.M. Forster, famous for his novel *A Passage to India*. After writing a rather critical review of the new novel, Father went on to read E.M. Forster's earlier novel, *A Passage to India* with a good deal of curiosity and interest. He was highly critical of both the English and Indian characters depicted by the author and, as for Dr Aziz, the hero of that novel, Father found him to be really offensive. A strong criticism of *A Passage to India* and its author was soon published in the *The Encounter*, which was edited by Stephen Spender, the poet. That critical piece of writing brought forth a strong rejoinder from K. Natwar Singh, the diplomat and who, many years later, would be the Minister for External Affairs, Government of India. Father replied to Natwar Singh's letter with a good deal of politeness and addressed him as Kanwar Sahib of Bharatpur. However, after meeting him at a guests' night at St Stephen's College, young Natwar Singh became a good friend of Father's, in spite of holding radically different political views.

Facing page: In the library with his pet cat, Kali Jhuli, presented to him by Melville de Mellow of All India Radio.

Discussing the difficulties he faced after leaving All India Radio with K. Natwar Singh and a friend, 1982.

Two important articles written by Nirad Chaudhuri were published in the summer of 1954, in *The Times* of London and *The Statesman* of Calcutta and New Delhi. The common topic of these two articles was controversial if not downright provocative in nature. The United States of America had agreed at that time to provide extensive military aid to Pakistan; that aid included the latest jet fighters such as the Saber and also

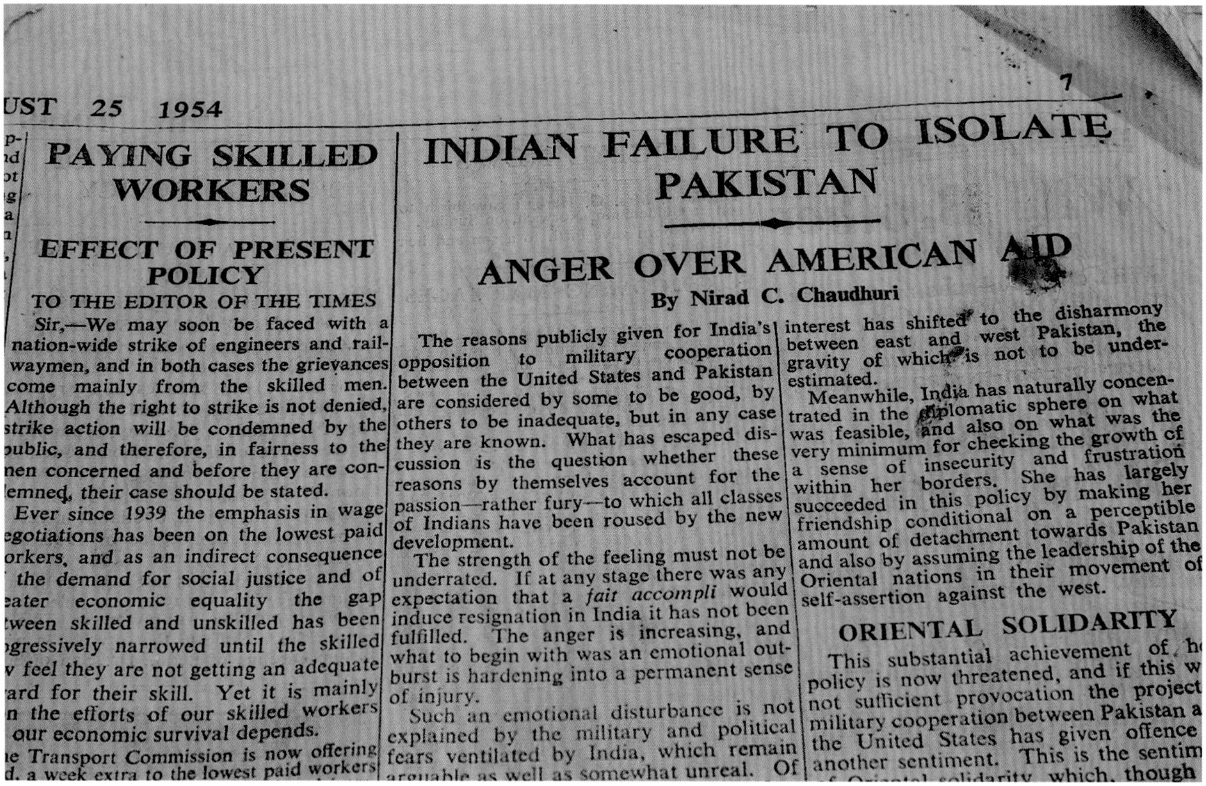

UST 25 1954 — 7

PAYING SKILLED WORKERS

EFFECT OF PRESENT POLICY

TO THE EDITOR OF THE TIMES

Sir,—We may soon be faced with a nation-wide strike of engineers and railwaymen, and in both cases the grievances come mainly from the skilled men. Although the right to strike is not denied, strike action will be condemned by the public, and therefore, in fairness to the men concerned and before they are condemned, their case should be stated.

Ever since 1939 the emphasis in wage egotiations has been on the lowest paid orkers, and as an indirect consequence the demand for social justice and of eater economic equality the gap tween skilled and unskilled has been ogressively narrowed until the skilled v feel they are not getting an adequate ard for their skill. Yet it is mainly n the efforts of our skilled workers our economic survival depends.

ie Transport Commission is now offering d. a week extra to the lowest paid workers

INDIAN FAILURE TO ISOLATE PAKISTAN

ANGER OVER AMERICAN AID

By Nirad C. Chaudhuri

The reasons publicly given for India's opposition to military cooperation between the United States and Pakistan are considered by some to be good, by others to be inadequate, but in any case they are known. What has escaped discussion is the question whether these reasons by themselves account for the passion—rather fury—to which all classes of Indians have been roused by the new development.

The strength of the feeling must not be underrated. If at any stage there was any expectation that a *fait accompli* would induce resignation in India it has not been fulfilled. The anger is increasing, and what to begin with was an emotional outburst is hardening into a permanent sense of injury.

Such an emotional disturbance is not explained by the military and political fears ventilated by India, which remain arguable as well as somewhat unreal. Of

interest has shifted to the disharmony between east and west Pakistan, the gravity of which is not to be underestimated.

Meanwhile, India has naturally concentrated in the diplomatic sphere on what was feasible, and also on what was the very minimum for checking the growth of a sense of insecurity and frustration within her borders. She has largely succeeded in this policy by making her friendship conditional on a perceptible amount of detachment towards Pakistan and also by assuming the leadership of the Oriental nations in their movement of self-assertion against the west.

ORIENTAL SOLIDARITY

This substantial achievement of h policy is now threatened, and if this w not sufficient provocation the project military cooperation between Pakistan a the United States has given offence another sentiment. This is the sentim of Oriental solidarity which, though

An article written by Nirad Chaudhuri that was published in The Times *of London, 25 August 1954.*

Patton tanks. Father, as a commentator on political and military affairs, argued that there was no real danger for India from the supply of mere military hardware to Pakistan. He suggested that all such threats should be counteracted with foreign policy decisions made at the highest level followed by modernising the defence force with weapons from other political blocks.

Then, on a cold January morning of 1955, Derek Holroyd, the BBC representative in India, sent a message to Father that he should meet Holroyd as soon as possible for an urgent proposal. On meeting him Holroyd informed Nirad Chaudhuri that the BBC was interested in four talks on England and, along with the British Council, was ready to finance a six-week visit to the country of his dreams—England. Apart from taking care of the airfare and all expenses while in England, the BBC offered to give him a handsome fee once these talks were broadcast.

That offer came as a dream come true for us and there was a lot of celebrating at home. However, Father got extremely upset after his first visit to the passport office. Extremely reluctant to face the hassles of getting all the formalities completed, he was practically on the point of giving up the idea of going to England till Mother took it upon herself to get everything done. Then, one early morning in March 1955, we almost pushed Father onto a BOAC Argonaut plane for his first journey to London.

Caught in a relaxed mood at the Palace Pier in London.

There was no telephone at our place at the time and international dialling services were unheard of. So when the first aerogramme written by Father arrived a few days later, we read about the excitement with which he first saw London from the air and also how he walked early next morning to the Westminster Bridge to see the view described by William Wordsworth. He was lodged at Bayswater and to reach the House of Parliament without asking for a single direction was a feat that only Nirad Chaudhuri could achieve with his meticulous study of guidebooks and maps, done long before he even dreamt of walking in London.

For the next six weeks we continued to receive letters from Father describing his visits to many notable places and events in England, including country houses as well as concerts and operas. But what was rather unexpected was his enjoyment of British food. He really went overboard after visiting some of the famous restaurants such as Wheeler's and Savoy Grill and having had lunch in clubs such as the Athenaeum.

After realising his dream of seeing many aspects of what Father later called 'Timeless England', he got an opportunity to visit Paris for two weeks. This unexpected windfall was possible thanks to the kindness of Count Ostrorog and the French Foreign Office. Following which Father spent three days in the ancient city of Rome, among the ruins of Forum Romanum, palazzos such as Borghese and Medici and fountains such as Trevi. Since this last leg of the journey was undertaken at his own expense, Father survived mainly on espresso coffee and croissants, and that too because he wanted to save money to buy an expensive cameo brooch for his wife.

Enjoying a light moment with French Ambassador Count Ostrorog and other friends, 1955.

The result of this short, yet deeply satisfying trip, was not only four outstanding talks for the BBC, but also a series of interesting features such as a 'Bengali on Pondezar' as well as the book *A Passage to England*, which went on to become a bestseller after being published in 1959. The money received from the BBC and from the sale of the book made it possible for Father to send Kirti to London University, where he got a first class Honours degree, the only student of history to get that distinction after his guide and professor, the famous historian Dr A.L. Basham.

After *A Passage to England* was widely acclaimed in England, Nirad Chaudhuri's position as an important writer and columnist came to be taken for granted. Even though I had taken up a job as a photographer at the School of Town & Country Planning,

Cutting a cake on his sixty-fifth birthday, Delhi, 1962.

now called the School of Planning and Architecture, the total family income was far from being adequate. At a meeting around this time, Khushwant Singh mentioned that the Government of India was not only prepared to lift the official ban on Nirad Chaudhuri, but also pay a large fee for writing a feature on refugees coming to India from East Pakistan. Father coolly replied that his own ban on the Indian Government continued and, after picking up his hat, walked out into the hot sun of the Delhi summer.

By the end of 1964 Nirad Chaudhuri had completed his next book, *The Continent of Circe*. However, this book got into difficulties with his first publisher Macmillan. Father was having serious problems with the attitude and views of the new French Ambassador who joined after Count Ostrorog died sometime in 1960 or 1961. Father decided to give up his job

A collection of Nirad Chaudhuri's books, both in Bengali and English.

at the French Embassy and complete a short monograph called *The Intellectual in India*. Very few people know about this interesting collection of essays. The publication rights were given away for a lump sum of money, thanks to the intervention of Professor Chinmoy Guha of Delhi University.

By then the good old Underwood typewriter could no longer withstand the strain of so much use and at times Father had to borrow a portable machine from Khushwant Singh. Later Sardar Sahib was kind enough to present him a brand new machine, enabling Father to type out the final version of *The Continent of Circe*. This timely help led to an interview in which Khushwant Singh is said to have mentioned that though Nirad Chaudhuri was the best non-fiction writer in India, he was still a poor man and did not even own a typewriter. Those words hurt Father and, even if somewhat misquoted by a woman journalist from the USA, he never expected such a comment from a close friend.

Even after becoming the author of three successful books published abroad, Nirad Chaudhuri had to face many financial uncertainties until he went on his second trip to England in 1967. It was only after this trip to receive the Duff Cooper Memorial Prize for Literature that Father's status as a financially independent author stabilised. That year he also completed his first Bengali book, *Bangali Jeevane Romoni* (Women in Bengali Life). The success of this book as well as some of the sensational articles he wrote for Bengali magazines and newspapers also contributed to Nirad Chaudhuri finally leading the life due to an eminent author.

The Road to Oxford

With his son, Kirti, at a country house in the United Kingdom, 1967.

The extraordinary rise in the stature of Nirad Chaudhuri as a writer and also an important intellectual and thinker came to be recognised soon after the award of the Duff Cooper Memorial Prize for Literature in early 1967. On receiving this prestigious prize from Field Marshal Auchinleck, Father, in his thanksgiving address, said, 'Literary prizes were always awarded to the wrong party, the author.' He added, 'A prize should really be awarded to the outstanding book, but by convention, was always misappropriated by the author.' This witty remark was greeted with cheers and a good deal of amusement and Father went on to compare himself to the role of Lord Ganesha writing the words of the epic *Mahabharata* for the sage Vyasa. He also quoted Michelangelo, who could see many of his sculptures hidden in blocks of uncut marble, even before he had made a single cut with his chisel.

After receiving the Duff Cooper prize, Father stayed on for a few weeks with Kirti in London. On the return flight to Delhi he took a stopover in Tel Aviv and made a whirlwind tour of Israel, thanks to a special invitation by the Government of that country. Unlike many other Indians of the time, Nirad Chaudhuri had openly supported the formation of Israel and had great admiration for that country and its people.

When we went to receive him, returning from this tour, one April morning at Palam Airport, which till then was still a collection of wartime barracks, his stride and words were both bold and happy. We could also see, sticking out of a duty-free bag, the golden foil wrapped around the neck of a champagne bottle, along with a wide paper roll, which looked like a map. Once in the car, Father announced that the champagne was no less than a Dom Perignon and the paper roll was actually a full-size reproduction of the nude Rockeby Venus by the famous Spanish painter, Velazquez.

Soon after reaching home at Mori Gate I was dispatched to Connaught Place to buy a refrigerator with the prize money that Father had brought back from London. A suitable golden frame had to be found for the proper display of the Venus. Both these items were needed in a hurry for a grand party that was being planned to celebrate the success of

Nirad Chaudhuri at a park in Oxford, 1971.

The Continent of Circe. The Dom Perignon was chilled to the correct degree with the ice made in the first refrigerator to come to our house, and the Venus looked gorgeous in its golden frame, against the backdrop of a beige velvet curtain. All the guests, European and Indian, could not but go back impressed. A few of the Indian guests had some problems looking at the nude Venus, especially after imbibing a couple of glasses of champagne!

Within a year's time there was a surprise once again for Father and Mother. Nirad Chaudhuri received an offer from Colonel Laurens Van der Post, then visiting Delhi and also from the Max Mueller family, to write a biography of the famous Vedic scholar, Professor Rt. Hon. Freidrich Max Mueller. The publishers, Chatto & Windus, were prepared to pay the air passage to England and all expenses for Father as well as Mother. It was too good an offer to be missed, so after a triumphant lecture tour of Calcutta, the first after coming away to Delhi in 1942, my parents left for London in May 1968.

Apart from staying at my brother's house in London and showing Mother all the classics of British culture, Father spent a good part of the six months at the university town of Oxford. The Bodleian Library in Oxford housed most of Professor Max Mueller's papers, many of them written by hand. These had been donated by his grandson J.H. Max Mueller. That visit was to be the beginning of my parents' long association with Oxford. It was here in two years time that the film-making duo of James Ivory and Ismail Merchant were to make an interesting documentary film for the BBC called *A Brown Man's Search for Civilisation*. In one of the more interesting scenes, Mother was shown feeding some swans on the bank of the River Isis at Oxford, while Father went on to address them in a chaste East Bengal dialect.

Amiya feeding birds at Cutteslowe Park, North Oxford, 1972.

After my parent's return from England, Father's seventy-first birthday was celebrated with much gusto. As chance would have it, it was combined with the first birthday celebration of my daughter Satarupa who, according to Father's preferred nomenclature,

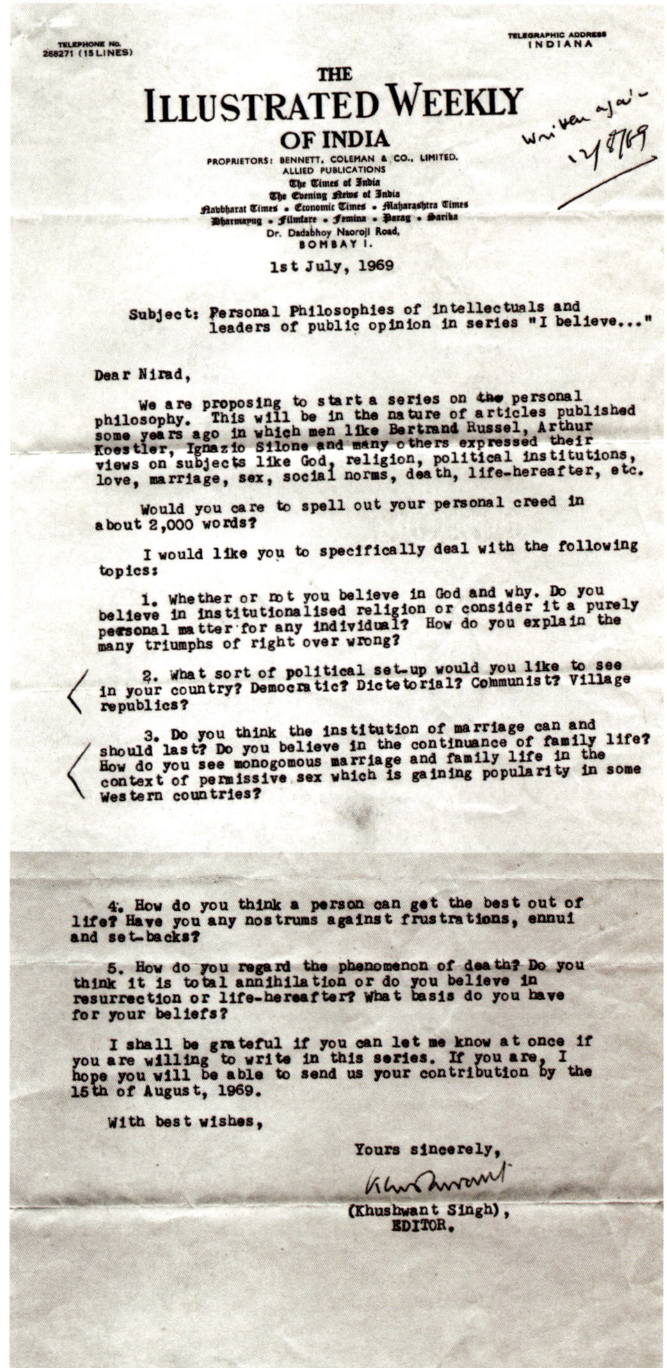

TELEPHONE No.
268271 (15 LINES)

TELEGRAPHIC ADDRESS
INDIANA

THE
ILLUSTRATED WEEKLY
OF INDIA

PROPRIETORS: BENNETT, COLEMAN & CO., LIMITED.
ALLIED PUBLICATIONS
The Times of India
The Evening News of India
Navbharat Times • Economic Times • Maharashtra Times
Dharmayug • Filmfare • Femina • Parag • Sarika
Dr. Dadabhoy Naoroji Road,
BOMBAY I.

1st July, 1969

Subject: Personal Philosophies of intellectuals and leaders of public opinion in series "I believe..."

Dear Nirad,

We are proposing to start a series on the personal philosophy. This will be in the nature of articles published some years ago in which men like Bertrand Russel, Arthur Koestler, Ignazio Silone and many others expressed their views on subjects like God, religion, political institutions, love, marriage, sex, social norms, death, life-hereafter, etc.

Would you care to spell out your personal creed in about 2,000 words?

I would like you to specifically deal with the following topics:

1. Whether or not you believe in God and why. Do you believe in institutionalised religion or consider it a purely personal matter for any individual? How do you explain the many triumphs of right over wrong?

2. What sort of political set-up would you like to see in your country? Democratic? Dictetorial? Communist? Village republics?

3. Do you think the institution of marriage can and should last? Do you believe in the continuance of family life? How do you see monogomous marriage and family life in the context of permissive sex which is gaining popularity in some Western countries?

4. How do you think a person can get the best out of life? Have you any nostrums against frustrations, ennui and set-backs?

5. How do you regard the phenomenon of death? Do you think it is total annihilation or do you believe in resurrection or life-hereafter? What basis do you have for your beliefs?

I shall be grateful if you can let me know at once if you are willing to write in this series. If you are, I hope you will be able to send us your contribution by the 15th of August, 1969.

With best wishes,

Yours sincerely,

(Khushwant Singh),
EDITOR.

Above: The Illustrated Weekly of India *cover, 1969;*
Right: Request from editor Khushwant Singh for an article.

was called Papagena. This weird name from Mozart's opera *Magic Flute* had begun as a joke when my daughter was born in December 1967 around the time that Father had presented me with a set of records of that opera.

Before one knew it two years had passed and no significant progress had been made regarding the biography of Max Mueller. Father's provocative writings in various newspapers and magazines and his flamboyant style of dressing had been causing many a storm at the fashionable New Delhi parties. Khushwant Singh intensified this storm into a cyclone when, as the new editor of *The Illustrated Weekly*, he published three articles by Father with the headline, 'Why I hate Indians'. The striking cover photograph in colour was taken by my friend and fellow photojournalist, T.S. Nagarajan and showed Nirad Chaudhuri in a maroon jacket with a fancy linen shirt trimmed with lace frills.

The three articles and the accompanying photographs created the usual furore all over India, boosting the sales of *The Weekly*. Special correspondents of the national dailies, along with representatives from some Indian publishers, rushed to Mori Gate and implored Father to write, promising a good amount to be paid as an advance. This well-deserved publicity resulted in two interesting but somewhat flippant books if one could call them that, *To Live or Not to Live* and *Culture in the Vanity Bag*. However, the first casualty of this popularity was the book on Max Mueller. Nirad Chaudhuri had hardly any time to complete the research let alone begin to write the book. With hordes of so-called friends and admirers dropping by at all odd hours, many of them even camping for days, no serious work could be done except for writing more than one newspaper column, which at that time was his main means for earning a livelihood.

And then there was another bolt from the blue. Like many other coincidences in Nirad Chaudhuri's life and career as an author, one fine morning in January 1970, the special correspondent of *The Times* rang up to say that Sir George Weidenfeld, Director of Weidenfeld and Nicholson publishers, wanted to meet Father at the earliest. That crucial meeting took place at the Oberoi Intercontinental; Sir George was keen that Father wrote a book on Hinduism for their series, 'Religions of the World'. The publishers were ready to finance my parents' complete expenses for flying to the UK and also their stay in that country for six months.

This proposal worked like magic for not only Father but everyone else as well. In June 1970, when we went to the airport to see them off, we were amazed to see the crowd of friends and admirers who had assembled at the check-in hall at Palam Airport. When my parents went aboard the VC-10 aircraft of British Airways, neither they, nor any of their well-wishers, had any inkling that this six-month stay in England would actually get extended to last the rest of their lives. In fact, Nirad Chaudhuri, who was approaching seventy-three at that time, would not be stepping on Indian soil again, a decision that he never consciously made.

After some uncertainties about my parents' return dates towards the end of 1970, Kirti, who was visiting Delhi, told us that Father

In Repertoire
From 19 April
From 26 April
The Tempest

had just moved to a cottage in the village Wheatley near Oxford. A few days later we got a letter from Mother and learnt that Father was assigned to write a book on Robert Clive after a dinner gathering at the Worcester College in Oxford. Actually Christopher MacLehose, Director of the publishing concern Barrie & Jenkins, also present at the Worcester College dinner, came to know from Mother that Father was planning to return to Delhi because of a lack of funds. Mother was very concerned that once they returned to India both the books on Max Mueller and Hinduism would get delayed, if not remain incomplete. Within a matter of a few days, the contract for his book on Clive followed with an advance.

More than two decades later, Nirad Chaudhuri admitted in an article written for *Desh* that the liability of writing those three books hung heavy on his conscience and could easily be compared to the plight of poor indigo farmers, as well as muslin weavers from Bengal, who could only survive on advances during the early British days in India. In a television interview in the late nineties, Father went on to say, 'I never asked for any of those writing assignments myself and nor did I seek any favour for coming and settling down in the UK as an immigrant.'

Facing page: Nirad Chaudhuri with Amiya outside a London theatre.

A view of Harefields, North Oxford, where the Chaudhuris lived.

But had Nirad Chaudhuri not received the offer at the Worcester College dinner to write about Clive, he would have been compelled to return to India. In fact, on the strength of this, Father was also generous enough to help me to go to the UK for doing a course on film and television as a medium of mass communication.

My first visit to England in the summer of 1971 was wonderful. I saw Oxford in the company of Father and attended a few cultural events in London with him. Our visit to the National Gallery, followed by a lunch at the Savoy Grill and a concert of Beethoven's music at the Royal Festival Hall, were experiences that have remained with me to this day.

As coincidence would have it, during my stay in England Nirad Chaudhuri received an invitation from the University of Chicago to deliver a series of lectures on Indian religion and culture, as a visiting professor. It was kind

Sir Hugo Brunner, Lord-Lieutenant for Oxford, who helped get Nirad Chaudhuri's Hinduism *published.*

of Professor Edward Shils to arrange this short teaching assignment in the USA for Father. A few months after his return from Chicago, Father got another teaching assignment in the USA, at the University of Austin in Texas. This visiting professorship came thanks to James Ivory and Ismail Merchant. My parents finally returned from Austin to Oxford in the late summer of 1972. After staying at a few temporary residences—Hollywell Hotel and a flat on Upper Fisher Row—they moved into 41 Harefields, a modern and comfortable flat in North Oxford.

The Max Mueller biography was completed here and published in 1974. Though *The Scholar Extraordinary* was acclaimed as a profound work, the book was hardly viable except in India, where in 1976 it got the Sahitya Academy Award in English literature. The next book was *Clive of India*. *Hinduism*, first commissioned by Weidenfeld & Nicholson, had run into serious difficulties because of the delay and would finally be published in 1979 by Chatto & Windus, owing largely to the efforts of Sir Hugo Brunner.

For a concise assessment about *Hinduism* and *Clive of India*, I can do no better than quote from an essay by Khushwant Singh in 'Not a Nice Man to Know': 'Nirad Chaudhuri's most serious book is *Hinduism*. It is not the platitudinous repetition of what one sees in other books on the subject: Vedas, Upanishads, Puranas, etc., but an altogether novel and refreshing approach to Hinduism as it is practised, and what it means to the average Hindu...Just about everything Nirad has to say on Hinduism will raise the hackles of orthodox Hindus, but none will be able to fault him on his facts. The book *Clive of India*,' added Khushwant Singh, 'was too much of a laboured attempt to defend a character, who most Indians regard as indefensible.'

It was certain that my parents would return to India once *Hinduism* was published in 1979; no other grant had come in till then. Father had been renewing the lease of the Harefields house after every six months since 1972. He had also retained the Mori Gate flat in Delhi for more than a decade. My parents were keen that my young daughter, then only eleven, should visit them before they leave Oxford and sent her an air ticket.

After remaining engrossed for about ten weeks in taking their granddaughter through the various facets of Britain and British culture that they loved so much, my parents began to think about ways of winding up their long stay in Oxford. It was a prospect that they did not look forward to. Apart from having to return to a congested locality in Old Delhi, the dilapidated condition of their flat and the problem of moving Father's large collection of rare books, pictures and antique china acquired abroad, appeared to be a daunting task.

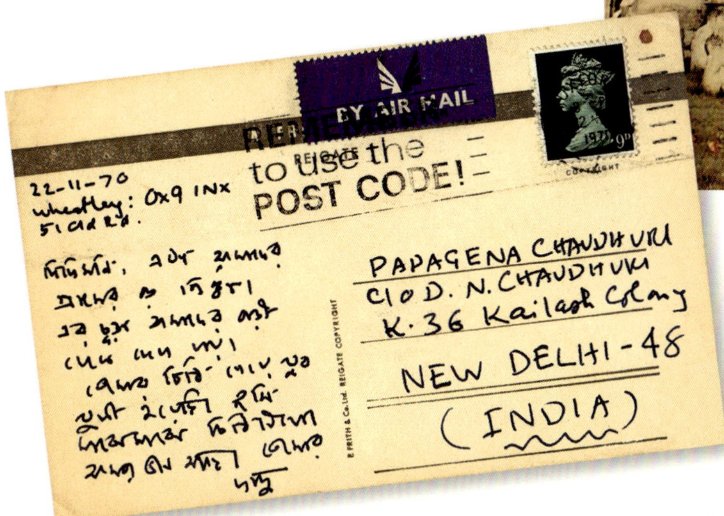

Postcard of a church in Oxford sent to his granddaughter Satarupa, affectionately called Papagena by him.

Nirad Chaudhuri working on his second autobiography, Thy Hand, Great Anarch!, *Oxford.*

Sometime in 1980 came another stroke of extraordinary luck for my parents. Thanks to the tireless efforts of Dr Gauhar Rizvi, then a young don at the University of Oxford, a generous social security pension for life was granted to my parents; that was the end of all financial difficulties for Father. At the age of over eighty years, he could now carry on with the writing of his second autobiography, *Thy Hand, Great Anarch!*, undisturbed.

The Triumphant Author

Dressed in formal wear, Nirad Chaudhuri entering his house on Lathbury Road, Oxford, 1993.

Once there was a steady flow of income from his social security pension, Nirad Chaudhuri began to concentrate on his book. But, as had happened many times in his life before, a sudden problem arose regarding the Harefields house. The owner probably developed cold feet after hearing that my parents had been granted a pension, which included a house rent of a substantial amount. So he initiated a court case to have the house vacated on the grounds of self-occupation. Father, instead of facing the trouble and expenses of prolonged litigation, agreed to vacate after one year. He also decided to wind up the old flat in Old Delhi and sent Mother to Delhi in early 1982 to do so. Mother, however, had to return to Oxford earlier than planned because of a rule she had overlooked on her return ticket. This change in her travel plan left me at the helm of completing a formidable wind-up operation.

Soon after Mother reached Oxford, it was decided that my wife Malabika, my daughter Satarupa and I would be going to Oxford for a summer holiday. Father felt that we should go to England before the large flat in Harefields was given up. As soon as our plan to visit the UK for three months was finalised, Father got tickets for us for a Shakespearean play at Stratford-Upon-Avon and for a concert at the Festival Hall in London!

When we arrived, Father came to meet us at Heathrow airport and appeared to be not a day older than when I had last seen him in 1971. From the very next morning, without making any concessions for our jet lag, we had to accompany a very enthusiastic father and grandfather to all his favourite spots around Oxford. These ranged from an old manor house beyond Cutteslowe Park to River Isis viewed from Christ Church Meadows and, of course, colleges such as Magdalen and Balliol. We were also taken to the Bodleian Library. Walking around the city centre, shops such as Selfridges and Marks & Spencer had his full approval while Debenhams and Littlewoods were considered frightfully cheap!

With Dhruva's wife, Malabika and their daughter Satarupa at a boat race in Oxford, 1982.

The lone reader, Nirad Chaudhuri, at the Bodleian Library in Oxford.

Father would be very excited to hear that we were going on conducted tours to places of great literary association such as Bath and Tintern Abbey. Though Father could not accompany us on our out-of-town weekend trips, he would trace our excursions on a detailed map and was as excited as us on our return and wished to hear of things in detail. After a most enjoyable ten-week summer holiday in England, my wife and daughter returned to New Delhi. By this time it was decided that my parents were to move to a house on Lathbury Road near Summer Town. I stayed back, therefore, to help them move to their new place, in early September.

Around that time, Alastair Niven, Director of the Commonwealth Institute in London, invited Father to make the opening presentation at a conference of Indian writers called, 'The Eye of the Beholder'. Mulk Raj Anand, Raja Rao, Anita Desai and Booker prizewinner Salman Rushdie were among the participants at this conference. Father took me along as a demonstrator, to exhibit a few of his school textbooks, an Indian almanac called *Panjika* and a large picture of the infant Shakespeare. These props helped Nirad

Nirad Chaudhuri was fond of a lavish lifestyle and always believed in eating well. Above: With a vintage bottle of wine. Right: Amiya serving lunch in the dining room, Lathbury Road, Oxford.

evian
evian
evian

Nirad Chaudhuri entering Iffley Church for the location shooting of a BBC film.

Chaudhuri talk about his early days in school and his familiarity with the English language and culture in the remote town of Kishorganj. As the presentation ended, there was a good deal of applause and mirth.

A few weeks later, there was a sudden proposal from the BBC for an hour-long film to be based on Father's book, *Hinduism*. Daniel Wolf, the producer of the *Everyman* series, came over to discuss that project. He was rather intrigued by Father's way of life and activities around Oxford. So instead of shooting indoor interviews alone, Daniel, after discussing it at length with me, decided to use various outdoor locations such as the Iffley Church, the old bookstore, Thornton's, as well as the main quadrangle of the Christ Church College. All of them were Father's favourite haunts in Oxford. The programme was aired sometime in 1983 and received much appreciation from both the viewers and the media alike.

By then my parents were well settled in their new house at 20 Lathbury Road. This typical Victorian building, with a large front garden and rooms laid out in the traditional English style, was the kind of house that Father had always dreamt of. Feeling very much at home, he set out to complete his last major work, *Thy Hand, Great Anarch!* A few months later, I came to know that the publishers had serious misgivings about this new book running into almost a thousand pages. Father was in no mood to change anything and withdrew the book from the publisher.

Finally, after a gap of almost two years, Graham Greene, then on the board of directors at Chatto & Windus, called for the manuscript

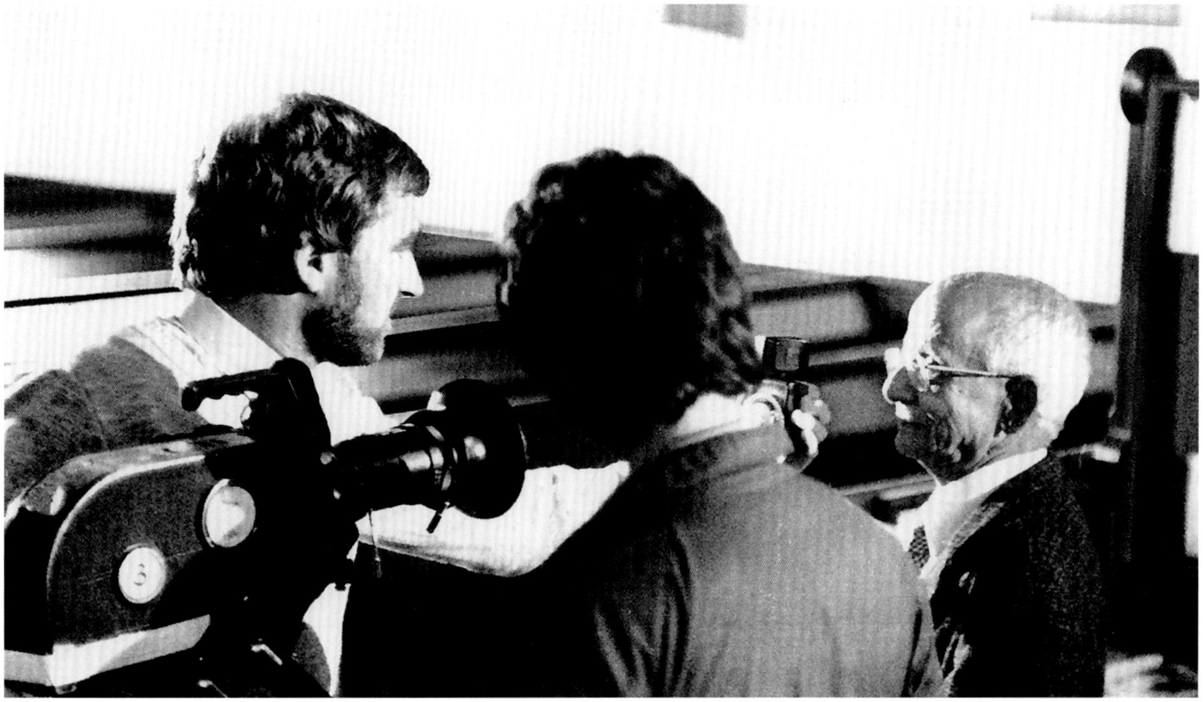

Nirad Chaudhuri conversing with a film crew from the BBC, 1982

once again and thanks to the intervention of Natwar Singh, *Thy Hand, Great Anarch!* was published both in the UK and the USA in November 1987 on Father's ninetieth birthday. Many of the reviewers not only considered this book an outstanding feat by a man touching ninety, but also an important record of happenings in India from 1922 to 1952. Surprisingly, one of the first recognitions for writing *Thy Hand, Great Anarch!* came from Calcutta. The Ananda Bazaar group of newspapers awarded the Ananda Purashkar (Ananda Prize) of 1988 to Father, and that too for an English work. Though Aveek Sarkar, Editor and Chief of the group, was extremely keen to have Father in Calcutta for the award presentation ceremony, the family physician in Oxford, Dr Mather, advised against long distance travel. So it was finally decided that I would represent Nirad Chaudhuri at the prize-giving ceremony held at the Grand Hotel in Calcutta. As chance would have it, on that very evening of 28 April 1988, Mother had her second heart attack. It was extremely fortunate that Father was there to call for medical help. Instead of getting us all alarmed with an immediate telephone call, Father posted a long letter, as was his habit,

Nirad Chaudhuri with the Ananda Purashkar award, 1988.

mentioning that Mother was coping well. Fortunately, I had already booked a ticket for the UK and would reach Oxford within two days of receiving that letter.

When I arrived at the Lathbury Road house the front garden was in a blaze of colour with all the spring flowers, including tulips, in full bloom. Father, dressed in a thick knitted pullover and a typical Bengali *dhoti*, was busy tending to his favourite collection of rhododendrons that had bloomed in several hues. The entire scene assured me that Mother must have recovered and probably returned home. After entering the house I was surprised to see her downstairs in the dining room, laying out a sumptuous lunch to celebrate my arrival after a gap of nearly six years. At the lunch table, I came to know that *Thy Hand, Great Anarch!* had been nominated for the prestigious 'National Cash Register' award for non-fiction books in London. Though the prize finally went to the widow of an English travel writer, the success of *Thy Hand, Great Anarch!* in sales as well as

Celebrating Amiya's eightieth birthday with their daughters-in-law and grandchildren, 1989.

publicity exceeded all expectations. In fact, my parents had to forgo a good part of their social security benefits for this. But Father could not care less as his second Bengali book, *Atmaghati Bangali* (Suicidal Bengalis), in spite of all the controversy it created, had been doing exceptionally well.

Mother, too, had begun to write her memoirs in Bengali. Every evening after a frugal dinner of soup and cottage cheese on toast or crackers she would write for about two hours, sitting near her bedside window upstairs. At times, when she felt that she had something that she would like to discuss, she would ring us up in Delhi and tell us about all that was happening at their end in Oxford. That is how the news came one night that the University of Oxford, in recognition of Nirad Chaudhuri's writings, had decided to award him an Honorary Degree of Doctor of Letters at its next Encaenia ceremony in March 1990. Mother was so excited that she wanted me to fly down to the UK at an early date.

Above: The University of Oxford in recognition of Nirad Chaudhuri's writings awarded him an Honorary Degree of Doctor of Letters, March 1990. Left: Amiya preparing snacks for the party after the ceremony.

The convocation was held at the Sheldonian Theatre in March 1990 and this was indeed a grand affair. In his speech in Latin, the public orator of the University said, 'The eminent Bengali whom I present is thoroughly versed both in English and European poetry and has interpreted Indian society and customs to us with great intellectual ability and skill. The Unknown Indian of his book has deservedly won fame and recognition.' It was a poignant moment to see Father draped in the scarlet red doctorate gown, receiving the Hon. Causa from Dr Lucas, the Vice-Chancellor of the University of Oxford. After the ceremony we had a wonderful celebration in our house. The most amazing thing about that high tea was that Mother had made everything herself, only two large cakes were ordered through her most obliging home-help.

Clockwise from top left: Draped in a doctorate gown, outside the Sheldonian Theatre with the Public Orator; Signing the honour's register at the convocation while Dr Lucas, Vice-Chancellor, University of Oxford, looks on; Formally entering the Convocation Hall; At the convocation lunch with Dr Lucas. Dhruva can be seen to his right.

Similarly, almost two years later, in 1992, came the news on telephone that Nirad Chaudhuri was being awarded the title of Honorary Commander of the British Empire (CBE). Since I had just returned from Oxford, I could not make it to the ceremony held in London. Recently, while browsing the internet, I came across a news item about this honour, which is reproduced below:

> 19 October 1992
>
> DR NIRAD CHAUDHURI BECOMES HONORARY CBE
>
> Peter Brooke, Secretary of State for National Heritage, announced today that Her Majesty the Queen has appointed Dr Nirad Chaudhuri an Honorary Commander of the British Empire (CBE).
>
> The award recognises the outstanding services he has rendered to British national life as a writer and journalist focusing on Britain's relationship

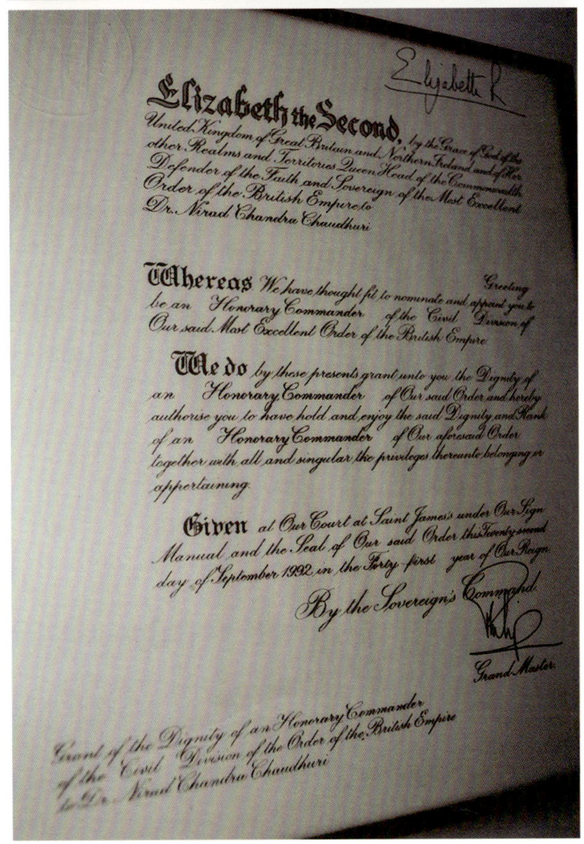

Elizabeth R

Elizabeth the Second, by the Grace of God of the United Kingdom of Great Britain and Northern Ireland and of Her other Realms and Territories Queen Head of the Commonwealth Defender of the Faith and Sovereign of the Most Excellent Order of the British Empire to Dr. Nirad Chandra Chaudhuri

Greeting

Whereas We have thought fit to nominate and appoint you to be an Honorary Commander of the Civil Division of Our said Most Excellent Order of the British Empire

We do by these presents grant unto you the Dignity of an Honorary Commander of Our said Order and hereby authorise you to have hold and enjoy the said Dignity and Rank of an Honorary Commander of Our aforesaid Order together with all and singular the privileges thereunto belonging or appertaining.

Given at Our Court at Saint James's under Our Sign Manual and the Seal of Our said Order this Twenty-second day of September 1992 in the Forty-first year of Our Reign

By the Sovereign's Command.

Grand Master.

Grant of the Dignity of an Honorary Commander of the Civil Division of the Order of the British Empire to Dr. Nirad Chandra Chaudhuri

Facing page: Nirad Chaudhuri at the convocation, Sterling University, Scotland; Top: At the ceremony where he was awarded the title of Honorary Commander of the British Empire (CBE) with Peter Brooke, British Secretary of State for National Heritage; Right: Document of the CBE honour signed by the Queen of England.

Film producer Rajiv Mehrotra shooting Nirad Chaudhuri at work, 1992.

with India. Mr Brooke will present the award to Dr Chaudhuri at a ceremony to be arranged. Mr Brooke said today: 'I congratulate Dr Nirad Chaudhuri on the bestowal of this honour. He is one of the great writers of this century in the English language. This award is a tribute both to Dr Chaudhuri and to his country.'

Around that time the documentary film producer Rajiv Mehrotra wanted to make a film on Father for Indian television, Doordarshan. Being a consultant on this project, it was time for me to be back in Oxford. My parents and I, along with Rajiv and his sound recordist, R. Kaul, had a memorable time shooting for the film at various locations around Oxford. The film was aired on Doordarshan in 1993 and also shown to a large and appreciative audience at the India International Centre in New Delhi.

Towards the Sunset, Alone

Amiya's death in 1994, following her brave battle with cancer, left him helpless and depressed.

On a frosty but bright morning in March 1994 my flight to Delhi had just taken off from Amsterdam's Schiphol airport. I was returning to India after another long visit to Oxford. Despite the courtesy and hospitality received on board the aircraft, I was still feeling depressed. The only reason for this could have been the deteriorating health condition of my mother. In the autumn of 1993 she had been diagnosed with cancer and had to now remain confined to her bedroom. Mother not only put on a brave front but went on controlling the affairs of the household just by using a cordless telephone. Between 1990 and 1994 she had managed to write, and also publish, a book on Indian cooking in English, as well as the two volumes of her autobiography in Bengali. Now she was writing the third part of her autobiography.

After I left Oxford, Mother would keep me regularly informed about what was happening there, including the progress of her book. During one of our telephonic conversations around the beginning of September 1994, she expressed her happiness over the fact that my daughter, who had chosen a career in editing and publishing of books, was about to join a major publishing concern associated with the University of Oxford. A few days later, all of

A rare informal photograph of Nirad Chaudhuri and Amiya in their bedroom, shortly before Amiya's death.

a sudden, there was a telephone call from Dr Tipu Aziz, a close family friend and a leading neurosurgeon of Oxford. He mentioned that Father, whom he called Dadu (grandfather), had something urgent to say. From the very tone of his voice I could guess that something had gone seriously wrong in Oxford. 'Your Mother passed away this morning! Come to Oxford as soon as you can.' That was all Father could manage to say and before I could utter a word the phone went dead in my hand.

Facing page: Nirad Chaudhuri with his three sons, Dhruva, Prithvi and Kirti, 1994.

My visa to the UK had just expired and in no way could I get it renewed that Saturday afternoon. It was not possible to fly out before the following Monday night. After informing my brother in Calcutta, I asked him to join me, if possible on the same flight. Fortunately for both of us, all the arrangements could be worked out mostly on the telephone and thanks to the officials of the British High Commission we could leave New Delhi on 19 September 1994.

Clockwise from top: Amiya busy at work, writing in her bedroom; Looking out from the window as she takes a break from reading the newspaper; Amiya on the telephone, photographed by Malabika Chaudhuri, 1991.

Shrabani Basu, the special representative of the Ananda Bazaar group, along with her husband Dipankar De Sarkar and sister Nupur Basu of NDTV, were there to receive us the next morning at Heathrow airport and drive us down to Oxford. On our way, Shrabani told us that the night before Mother passed away she had appeared to be quite cheerful and had gone on talking with Father late into the night. Early next morning, when Father had come upstairs with her usual cup of malted milk, Mother was in great discomfort and seemed to be having a heart attack. She passed away within a few minutes, after Dr Aziz reached our house. 'Who will look after you when I am gone?' Those were the last words that my mother could utter.

We reached Oxford to find Father shattered but as voluble as ever. Our family friends, Dr and Mrs Pal Chaudhuri from Cardiff, were already there to look after him. The funeral was held two days after our arrival. Father refused to go to the crematorium near Oxford; he just touched the flower-decked

Cleaning rice for his lunch, shortly after the death of Amiya.

coffin inside the hearse and walked slowly back to the house supported by Gopal Krishna Gandhi, then Director of the Nehru Centre, London and the diminutive Shrabani Basu.

Late in the evening, when everyone had left, he lapsed into a glum silence once again. He began to repair the frame of a lithograph depicting the Qudsia Bagh of Old Delhi done by one of the Daniels. Prithvi and I left the drawing room, realising that perhaps Father was going back to those memories of 1945 when he went for morning walks with Mother—Qudsia Bagh was their favourite spot. Suddenly there was a crashing sound from the next room and also the shattering of glass. After rushing in we found that Father had tried to put up that heavy framed picture on the wall all by himself. Fortunately he escaped with only a minor injury in his leg. But, from the next day onwards, Father kept moving the heavy furniture upstairs from one spot to another to set up a memorial for his late wife.

After completing the formalities at the social security office as well as making arrangements for a daily home-help for Father, I returned to New Delhi in late November 1994 to fulfil an urgent teaching assignment. On my next trip to Oxford in June 1995 I found Father had adjusted well to being alone in the house and kept himself busy with his English and Bengali writings. His last English book, *Three Horsemen of the New Apocalypse*, was progressing well and the second volume of his essays on Rabindranath Tagore was ready to be published by Mitra & Ghosh of Calcutta. During my visit I prepared some of his favourite European and Bengali

Engrossed in writing Three Horsemen of the New Apocalypse, *1995.*

dishes. It was also necessary to compile a collection of his articles written for English newspapers and magazines and bring them out in the form of a book. On my next two visits to Oxford, in the spring and autumn of 1996, I found that the celebrity status of Nirad Chaudhuri had reached such a peak that relatives and friends (who were nowhere on the horizon during his difficult days) and also politicians were making a beeline for the Lathbury Road house. Some were bold enough to even demand a signed copy of one of his books for free.

Father continued to be absorbed in his writings, as well as in listening to music, mostly Tagore songs. In autumn, the horse chestnut trees of North Oxford had turned yellow. The profusion of golden leaves strewn all over Lathbury Road and the garden path appeared to be in complete harmony with Father's thoughts and writings about the inevitable cycle of life and death as the final destiny of man.

In *Three Horsemen of the New Apocalypse*, Nirad Chaudhuri, nearing hundred years of his life, described the final fate of mankind. He compared it to living in an immense palace with radial aisles leading to a central hall. There the mysterious figure of Death stood with his face hidden and, once revealed, would clasp every individual to its bosom.

Reading the fine script with the help of a magnifying glass, 1996.

In the last Bengali article, which I saw him writing on my visit in 1997, Father went one step further regarding his own philosophy about life and death. To illustrate his point, he quoted Marcus Aurelius, the Roman Emperor from the second century: 'Mortal man you have been a citizen in the great City [Polis], and what does it matter for five or fifty years.' Later, the same monarch concluded: 'Leave the stage, therefore, and be reconciled for He, also who, lets his servant depart is reconciled.' In the same piece of his writing Father mentioned that he could conquer the fear of death only by surrendering to the inevitability of death. Like Tagore, Nirad Chaudhuri believed that he had carried death all along his life. But, differing from Tagore on an important point, Father concluded that there was no glorious life after death and that it was the final end.

At the ceremony where he was presented the Desikottama degree, London, 1997. Photograph courtesy Satarupa.

It was perhaps ironical that after contradicting many of the significant philosophical thoughts propounded by Tagore, Father in the last few years of his life called him the greatest of all Bengalis. A complete chapter on Tagore in *Thy Hand, Great Anarch!* went a long way to support this view. For the last few years of his life Father was also completely immersed in Tagore's short stories and songs; he quoted them often as examples portraying the great Bengali culture of the nineteenth and twentieth centuries. It was, therefore, no surprise that the Vishwa Bharati University of Santiniketan decided to bestow the highest honorary degree, Desikottama, on Nirad Chaudhuri. The presentation function was held at the Nehru Centre in London. On 2 August 1997, Father attended that ceremony dressed in a *dhoti* and kurta, along with the red robe of the Oxford University draped over his shoulder. The blue CBE medal conferred by the Queen of England could clearly be seen fastened to a chain around his neck.

Previous pages: Walking in the snow-laden garden at Lathbury Road, 1994; Top left to right: With the former President of India R. Venkataraman; At home, wearing his CBE medal.

I could not be present at this occasion on account of work in Delhi, but my daughter Satarupa spent a few weeks in Oxford and London at the time. After giving us a vivid account of that occasion, she mentioned how her grandfather's remark about having been a writer in English and not an Indian writer of English had created a commotion among the audience. Later, some people, including a few literary figures from Calcutta, were quite vocal about Father being honoured by the Vishwa Bharati University. They wrote strongly against this decision in a few newspapers and magazines. Little wonder, then, that Nirad Chaudhuri, like many of his famous Bengali predecessors, though disappointed and bitter about the literary circles of Calcutta, had been fortunate that something quite inexplicable had moved him on to Delhi and later to Oxford.

Touching a Century

Cutting the cake on his hundredth birthday, assisted by Dhruva, 1997.

On a cold and dreary evening in November 1997, I boarded an express coach from Heathrow to Oxford. I was going to arrange and take part in Nirad Chaudhuri's centenary celebrations, less than three weeks away. The approach of that memorable day should have made me and the others who were going to take part in the celebration happy; yet as I looked out of the coach window at the English countryside, the bleak winter landscape seemed to be in tune with my thoughts, which were rather low, if not downright sad. Father had sounded quite ill when I had talked to him on the telephone the previous evening. He was coughing incessantly and could hardly speak clearly. He also seemed to be quite upset with the news that some prominent people of Calcutta, including a few literary figures, were critical about the honour, Desikottama, conferred on him by the Vishwa Bharati University.

As my coach was approaching Oxford, which had become almost like my second home since 1988, it occurred to me that very few people understood that the only way I could raise the passage money for looking after Father was by compiling and editing many of his old articles for publishing as books. No less than seven such books in both English and Bengali were published between 1995

An exterior shot of the Lathbury Road house on a beautiful autumn day.

and 1999. Those books were the only records of what Nirad Chaudhuri wrote for leading newspapers and magazines for seventy years from 1926 to 1996. Most of them also proved to be an extensive documentation as well as an important commentary on the socio-political happenings in India and also in countries such as the UK and the USA. Initially reluctant about republishing his old writings, Father was nevertheless happy in the end to see many of his old articles published in the form of books.

When I reached Lathbury Road, the large house appeared to wear a dark and gloomy look. After entering the drawing room, I saw Father lying huddled on a sofa, almost dangerously touching the gas-fired hearth of the sitting-room. Except for a small table lamp in a corner, that room had hardly any other light. Father tried to sit up on hearing me open the door, but appeared to be so weak that he could hardly utter a word or two in greeting; he also appeared to be running a temperature. It was quite an uphill task for me, along with a family friend who had offered to help and more than one doctor in attendance, to make Father somehow recover before his birthday celebrations that were scheduled a few weeks away.

The scenario was aptly described by two expatriate journalists, Suman Buchar and Amit Roy, in a piece that they sent in from London to *The Telegraph*, published by the Ananda Bazaar group in Kolkata: 'In the last

THE HOUND OF THE BASKERVILLES

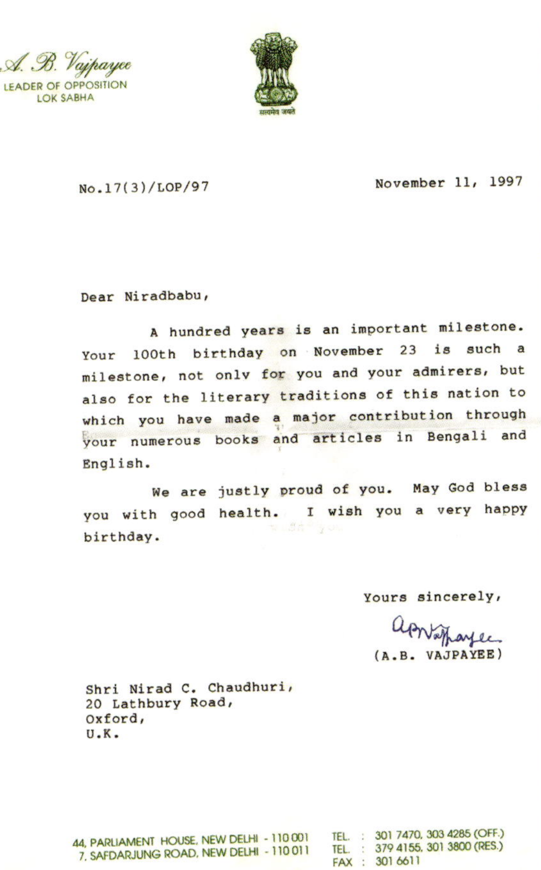

A. B. Vajpayee
LEADER OF OPPOSITION
LOK SABHA

No.17(3)/LOP/97

November 11, 1997

Dear Niradbabu,

A hundred years is an important milestone. Your 100th birthday on November 23 is such a milestone, not onlv for you and your admirers, but also for the literary traditions of this nation to which you have made a major contribution through your numerous books and articles in Bengali and English.

We are justly proud of you. May God bless you with good health. I wish you a very happy birthday.

Yours sincerely,

(A.B. VAJPAYEE)

Shri Nirad C. Chaudhuri,
20 Lathbury Road,
Oxford,
U.K.

44, PARLIAMENT HOUSE, NEW DELHI - 110 001
7, SAFDARJUNG ROAD, NEW DELHI - 110 011
TEL. : 301 7470, 303 4285 (OFF.)
TEL. : 379 4155, 301 3800 (RES.)
FAX : 301 6611

Left to right: A letter from A.B. Vajpayee; With Professor Indra Nath Choudhuri, Director, Nehru Centre.

few days at Nirad C. Chaudhuri's home in Lathbury Road, Oxford, doctors have been coming and going. His son Dhruva who has flown from Delhi for the third time in a year was not confident that his father would make it to Sunday the twenty-third of November…In between breathless coughing Nirad Babu demanded a pen and paper from Dhruva. With difficulty he scrawled the words: Have you read John Gross? He was thrilled with the favourable review of *Three Horsemen of the New Apocalypse*, which had appeared on that very day in the *Sunday Telegraph* published from London.'

Facing page: All ready to leave for the hundredth year celebrations at Trinity College.

With author Vikram Seth, Alastair Niven, Head of Literature, British Council and his wife.

And this is what John Gross had written: 'Next Sunday Nirad Chaudhuri will be celebrating his hundredth birthday. His latest work was written during his ninety-ninth year, a feat which no doubt qualifies for a place in *The Guinness Book of Records*. The three horsemen of his title represent individualism, nationalism and democracy. He has an interesting comment to make on all three.'

In the same dispatch Amit and Suman went on to write: 'If Nirad Babu is strong enough, his son intends to take him to a lunch party, which is being co-hosted by two old friends, Alastair Niven, Head of Literature at the British Council and Sir Hugo Brunner, who as Lord-Lieutenant for Oxford would represent the Queen. The lunch is being held at Trinity College, Oxford, where Brunner is a fellow. On the guest list are Dr Colin Lucas, Vice-Chancellor of Oxford University, Vikram Seth, the famous novelist, Professor Indra Nath Choudhuri, Director of the Nehru Centre in London,

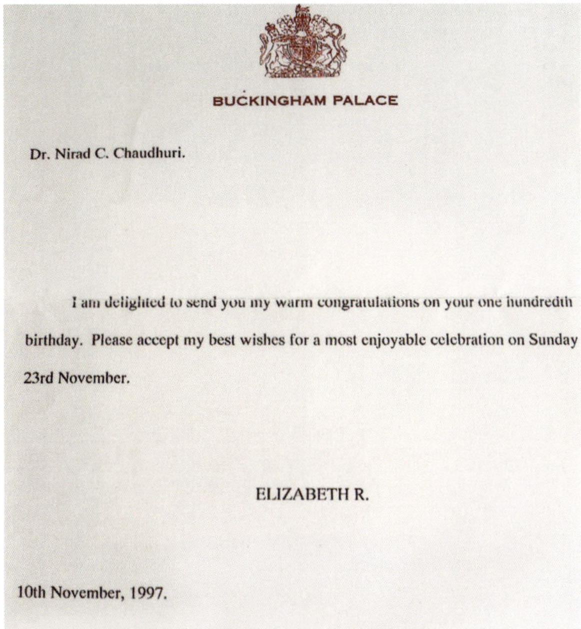

BUCKINGHAM PALACE

Dr. Nirad C. Chaudhuri.

I am delighted to send you my warm congratulations on your one hundredth birthday. Please accept my best wishes for a most enjoyable celebration on Sunday 23rd November.

ELIZABETH R.

10th November, 1997.

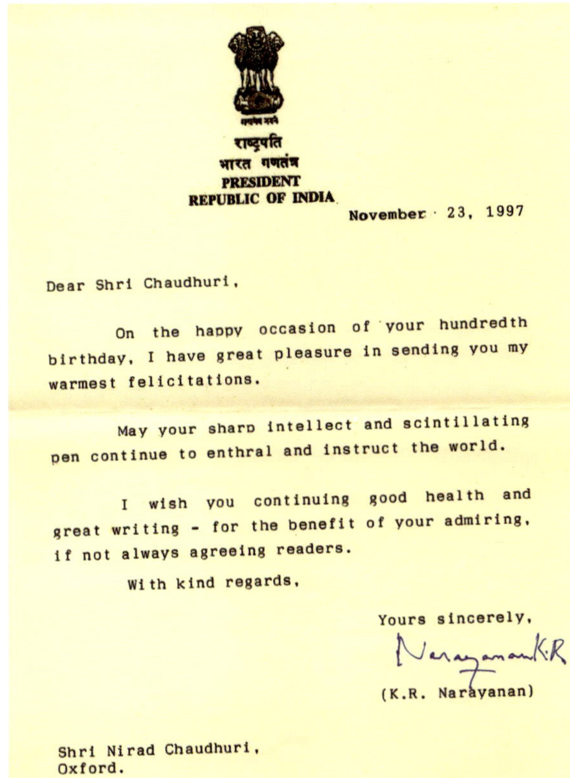

राष्ट्रपति
भारत गणतंत्र
PRESIDENT
REPUBLIC OF INDIA

November 23, 1997

Dear Shri Chaudhuri,

On the happy occasion of your hundredth birthday, I have great pleasure in sending you my warmest felicitations.

May your sharp intellect and scintillating pen continue to enthral and instruct the world.

I wish you continuing good health and great writing - for the benefit of your admiring, if not always agreeing readers.

With kind regards,

Yours sincerely,

Narayanan K.R

(K.R. Narayanan)

Shri Nirad Chaudhuri,
Oxford.

Congratulatory messages from the Queen of England and the President of India.

and the well-known editor Jeremy Lewis who also happened to be the editor of *Thy Hand, Great Anarch!*'

Having struggled between life and death for a fortnight, Nirad Chaudhuri got well enough to finally join the celebrations at Trinity College, even though for a brief period. And for the first time in his life he was compelled to use Mother's abandoned wheelchair. He was dressed formally, complete with a bow tie and the full regalia of his red gown and the blue-and-gold of the CBE medal. Sir Hugo read out a message from the Queen: 'I am delighted to send you my warm congratulations on your hundredth birthday. Please accept my best wishes for a most enjoyable celebration on Sunday, 23 November 1997.' It was signed Elizabeth R, the letter R standing for 'Regina'. The message from the then President of India, the late Dr K.R. Narayanan, stated, 'May your sharp intellect and scintillating pen continue to enthrall and instruct the world. I wish you continuing good health and great writing for the benefit of your admiring, if not always agreeing, readers.'

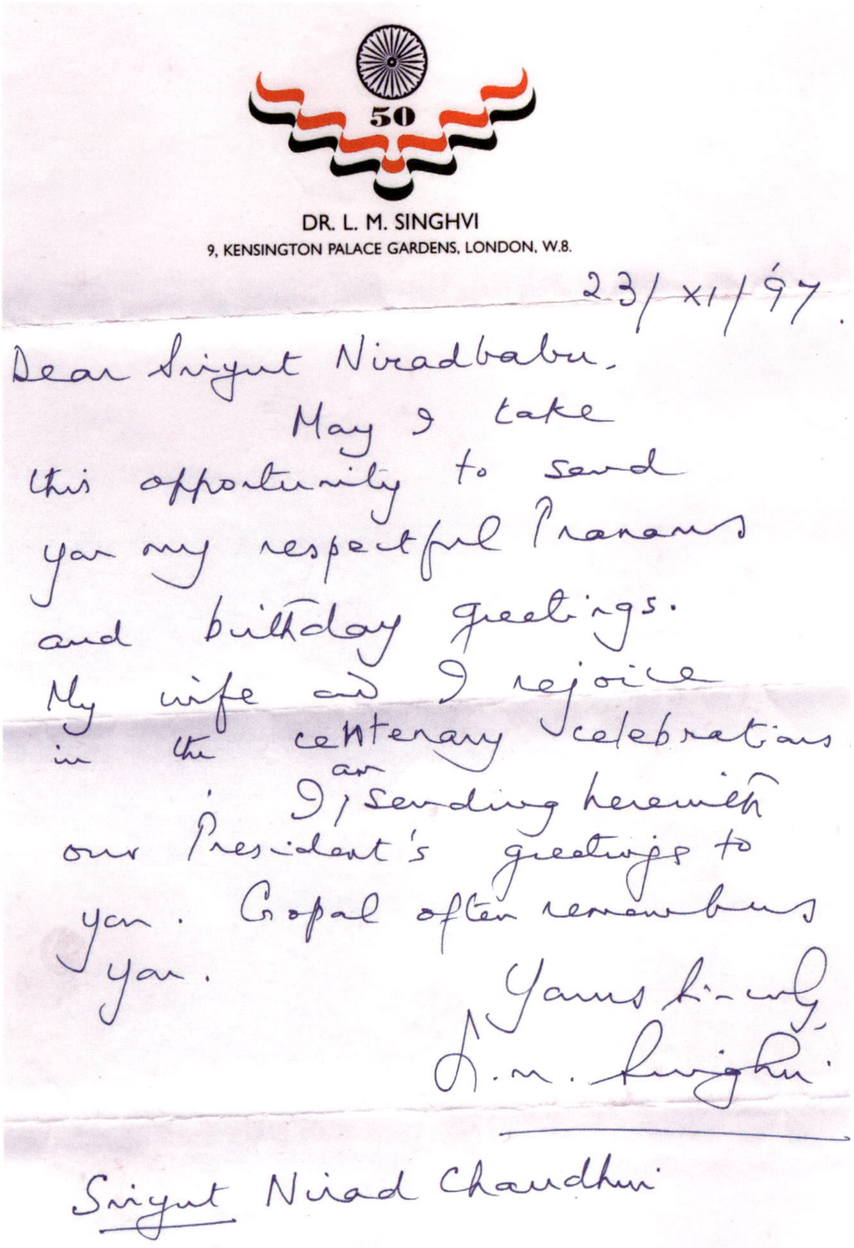

DR. L. M. SINGHVI
9, KENSINGTON PALACE GARDENS, LONDON, W.8.

23/XI/97.

Dear Srijut Niradbabu,

May I take this opportunity to send you my respectful Pranams and birthday greetings. My wife and I rejoice in the centenary celebrations. I am sending herewith our President's greetings to you. Gopal often remembers you.

Yours sincerely,
L. M. Singhvi

Srijut Nirad Chaudhuri

High Commissioner Dr L.M. Singhvi's greetings to Nirad Chaudhuri on the centenary celebrations.

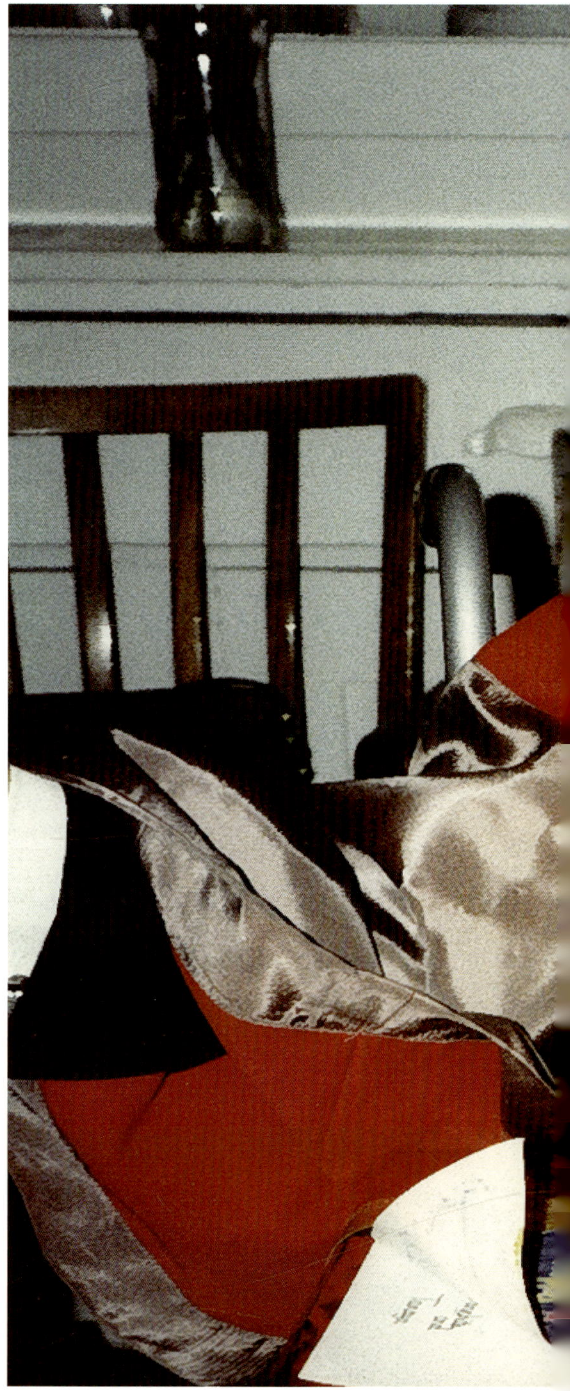

Alastair Niven addressing guests, including Professor Indra Nath Choudhuri and journalist Amit Roy.

Alastair Niven, after proposing a toast in Telmont Brut champagne, said: 'One hundred years from now, people will be reading *The Autobiography of an Unknown Indian, Thy Hand, Great Anarch!* and other books, and marvel about the author.' Father replied to all those greetings and also to the toasts in Latin as well as English. Then, after taking a few sips of the vintage champagne, he was seen off at the gate of Trinity College by a procession of guests, as proposed by Vikram Seth and seconded by the Vice-Chancellor.

In the evening, family friends—including those from the world of publishing and the media—were invited to Lathbury Road to celebrate in a less formal manner and in a somewhat Bengali ambience. For a true picture, both verbal and pictorial, I have to depend on the kindness of Shrabani Basu for her dispatch published in *Ananda Bazaar Patrika*, as well as photographs taken by her and her husband. I must also acknowledge the gift of a resplendent bouquet and two huge birthday cakes sent by the Ananda Bazaar group of publications. Those cakes were from Fortnum & Mason and had 'Happy 100th Birthday' written in both the English and Bengali scripts.

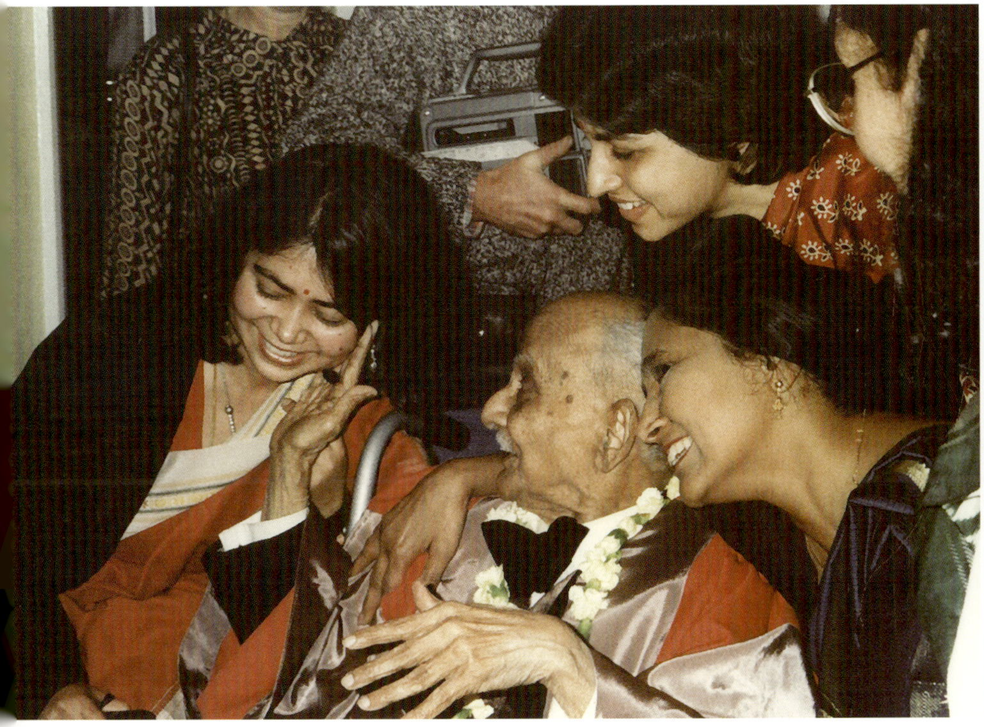

With Shrabani Basu, Gopa Majumdar and Krishna Dutt.
Pictures courtesy Shrabani Basu.

Father, once again dressed up for the occasion, appeared in a wheelchair and, in spite of the affectionate greetings and merrymaking around him, appeared to be rather subdued. He was clearly missing Mother; he had also not quite reconciled himself to the use of a wheelchair. After he had cut the two cakes and tasted the Bengali birthday preparation, *payesh*, a little girl (Shrabani's young daughter) garlanded Father. Many bottles of Dom Perignon champagne, received from an anonymous admirer, were popped open and a toast for Nirad C. Chaudhuri was proposed for having completed a hundred years. Father felt tired after all the emotional expressions of the moment and he had to retire to an improvised bedroom on the ground floor to rest.

He, however, returned to the dining-hall later, where Vikram Seth, Sir Hugo Brunner, Alastair Niven, Professor and Mrs Thomas, Gopa Majumdar and Krishna Dutt, both authors, were all happily gathered. I was playing the role of a substitute host. Once Father began to recite Matthew Arnold's poem *Scholar Gypsy* to illustrate his own life, everyone cheered with great gusto to the

Having seen Paco Pena's Flamenco Dance Company, WILLIAM RADICE writes a poem for Nirad C Chaudhuri's 100th birthday which he hopes to read out at a lunch in Oxford today

A sonnet for Mr Chaudhuri

Too slight in frame to dance with pounding feet,
Instead you stamped and strutted with your mind,
Imposed your pulse on history's failing beat,
Made truth from passion, reason, wit combined.
You suffered for your knowledge, scanned too wide
Our sinking world, our dreary cosmic fate;
Yet faith in a "great mercy" on the side
of those "unfittest" said, Create, create!
And whirling books emerged that proudly flung
Ripples of thought like rattling castanets.
Decadence never touched the song you sung;
Your vigour even your hundred years forgets!
Like fiery Shiva stamping out the world,
Life is the beat to which your dance has twirled

Clockwise from left: Poem by William Radice; Cover of Desh, *November 1997, painting based on a photograph by Dhruva; Covers of three of the five books edited by Dhruva.*

accompaniment of the flashing of many cameras and video sun-guns. Vikram Seth exclaimed that this birthday celebration was one of the most memorable experiences of his life.

The last remark Nirad Chaudhuri made to all well-wishers and friends that evening was that it had been wonderful to see the first signs of daylight earlier that morning and to realise that he had finally completed a century in his life. Father once mentioned to Shrabani in an interview: 'I cannot control death. I may live to be a hundred-and-ten, or die tomorrow. There is nothing certain about death at all.' That dispatch concluded by saying. 'The chronicler of this century and older to it by three years, Nirad C. Chaudhuri can now sit back after having observed and enjoyed the happiest of his birthdays in his life.'

Postscript

Those Oxford Days...

Eleven-year-old Satarupa during her summer vacations in 1979, which she spent with her grandparents in England.

An author, an editor, a journalist, a social and political commentator, a critic, a scholar, a broadcaster, a connoisseur, NCC had many facets to his personality but no matter what, to me, he always remained a grandfather first. Despite the many quizzes, some of them of a high literary order, often faced straight off the flight from Delhi or faced time and again during the vacations spent with Grandma and him in Oxford, he remained a person with whom there was a great sense of sharing, of good humour, good cheer and an incredible joie de vivre.

Nirad Chaudhuri with Satarupa, who shared a special bond with her grandfather.

When I embarked on this journey of retrospection, though somewhat hesitantly at first, it was reassuring to find memories come flooding back and to be suddenly transported to another time and place or to be more precise to several times and places, all bound together by the same thread—Grandfather!

I remember a particular summer vacation, I was aged eleven and it was my first-ever trip to England, Grandfather was eighty-one, and the mission was to share as much as possible of the 'timeless England' that he loved so well. We visited the numerous colleges in Oxford, taking our time to admire the quadrangles, the chapels, the ivy on the walls and the ancient trees that grew within the environs. We visited the Sheldonian Theatre, the Bodleian Library, walked in the Christ Church meadows and followed the path that led to the riverside. We went to see Shakespeare's birthplace in Stratford, Anne Hathway's cottage nearby and to numerous little towns and villages in the Cotswolds. We went to London to watch Rudolph Nureyev in Tchaikovsky's *Sleeping Beauty*, to listen to Handel's *Messiah* at the Royal Festival Hall, to Westminster Abbey, the National Gallery, the British Museum and the Natural History Museum. We also went aboard a paddle-steamer anchored on the Thames. This was en route to a visit to one of his publishers—Chatto and Windus.

Everywhere we went there were anecdotes upon anecdotes, notes on the historicity of

With his stick and granddaughter for company, Nirad Chaudhuri enjoyed his walks.

the place, pointers to the architecture and the natural history. There was much indulgence too…when I wanted to try out all the do-it-yourself experiments at the Natural History Museum not only was I encouraged to do so but Grandpa himself had a go at many of them and we had a neat competition going as to who would manage a better timing than the other. Many of these visits were day trips out from Oxford, so right from railway and coach tickets to timings and directions, everything was chalked out well beforehand with the precision of a general going into battle, and these were not the times of the internet!

Very little went wrong on these trips except perhaps the blowing off of a granddaughter's hat by the mighty gusts of the London Underground and one other incident which I'll relate in just a while. To return to the hat, the moment it blew off it was almost a foregone conclusion that it would be lost forever to the labyrinths of the London Tube, but for a short brisk run along a platform on the Bakerloo line, a sprightly leap in the air

Discovering beautiful parks and gardens—Satarupa with her mother and grandfather, Oxford.

and the hat had been recovered…by an agile young man of eighty-one—Grandpa!

The timeless England for me, and definitely for him, lay as much in some of the sights and sounds described above as in an even closer and more tactile contact with the earth. We would visit a friend's farm near Lambourn and stop to talk to the sheep, the horses and the geese wherever possible. We would go up the hill to take a closer look at the three thousand-year-old Uffington White Horse etched in chalk on the White Horse Hill. Wherever we would visit, sooner rather than later we would find ourselves stopping by a river, a lake or a pond, sometimes to munch on the delicious sandwiches made by Grandma, sometimes to share these with the ducks and geese vociferously quacking in the vicinity, sometimes to discuss how the weeping willow and the island in the middle of the pond shielded these ducks and geese from foxes at night, sometimes to see university students practising for Eight Weeks, sometimes to see a barge or a tugboat, at others to simply sit on the banks of the Cherwell at the Botanical Gardens and watch the punts go by.

The Isis and the Cherwell at Oxford, the Thames in London, the Avon in Stratford, it was only many years later that I'd learn about Grandpa's fascination for rivers but at the time it seemed to be the most natural thing to do. It was also most natural to potter about with Grandpa as he worked in his garden proudly showing off his rhododendrons one year, his climbing roses, crocuses and tulips the next. Whether he lived in Harefields or on Lathbury Road, the garden would remain an elemental and integral part of his life as much as his writing. An ancient horse chestnut that stood in one corner of the 20 Lathbury Road garden would often be an object of quiet contemplation for him and a signal for the change in seasons. The antics of the wood pigeons inhabiting that particular tree would never fail to raise a chuckle from him.

Apart from the flowers, bushes and trees he tended to so carefully, he always had a patch of mint and parsley because Grandma wanted them fresh from the garden for the varied culinary delights that she would conjure up—the kedgeree amongst them being my personal favourite. He would get his garden tools out of the shed and do all the necessary digging and planting himself, sometimes huffing and puffing if it was a hot summer's day but always confident that he could outdo youngsters like me who began to huff and puff much before he did. We would drag out an enormous hose-pipe between us, connect it to a tap and start watering the garden while he

Satarupa going through family photographs and letters with Nirad Chaudhuri, while her mother looks on.

explained his interest in all things botanical including why exactly he stored a bag of peat in the garden shed. We would occasionally come across a surprised looking hedgehog in the garden who would then scuttle away shyly.

It was this very strong connection with nature that drew NCC to walk through the countryside around Oxford for miles every day for many, many years. During the course of my first visit to Oxford, Grandpa and I set off on a walk early one morning. It was around 6 am, late for Grandpa but there were concessions to be made for a grandchild of eleven. We walked down the entire stretch of Harefields—where they lived in those years.

Satarupa enjoying the swings at Cutteslowe Park, which she visited with her grandfather.

We then followed various twists and turns in the road till we arrived at Cutteslowe Park, Grandpa in his tweeds and deerstalker, walking stick in one hand, his favourite grey bag in the other. In the bag he usually carried the A-Z when we went to London, various eatables, maps and pamphlets and a pair of binoculars. All was well, it was a bright sunny summer morning—the sky was very blue, there were stray wisps of fluffy white clouds, we went past the swings, I demanded that I have a go on them, this was acceded to, the mighty horse chestnuts were pointed out—a pink and a white in full bloom. We reached the pond with the weeping willow and stopped to see what the geese were doing. Then we walked on to the far end of the park, which bordered a natural grassy green football field spotted with sparkling white daisies, the players were nowhere in sight, we walked on across the field, then past some bushes till we came to a stile—of roughly hewn wood—step up, step across and step down, the blackbirds were singing,

Satarupa discovered many places in timeless England, with her grandfather as her guide.

a field of corn lay ahead, we walked through the field following a little path, a picture of breathtaking beauty, Grandpa pointing out a bird here, a tree there. A while later he pointed in a particular direction with his stick saying, 'We'll go as far as Water Eaton and then turn for home.' We had been walking for well over an hour by then and the sun had climbed higher in the sky. Despite the beauty of the Arnoldian countryside, Grandpa's statement of intent wasn't greeted by much enthusiasm from me. On the contrary I declared that I wanted some water to drink! NCC swiftly dug into the grey bag but misfortune of misfortune no bottle of water could be found, no lemonade either...normally he would always carry these on our trips out but it has to be conceded that every general has his day off! We turned back for home, the pace was slow, Grandpa couldn't insist on the brisk pace he usually commanded, on reaching the stile the granddaughter sat down on it and refused to budge further till water was fetched! The twinkle in the

Satarupa in an animated conversation with Nirad Chaudhuri at his Harefields house.

granddaughter's eye was completely missed by Grandfather—his predicament was severe, he couldn't possibly go home and return with the water—it was too far for that, there were no handy stalls nearby that sold any kind of a drink so there was nothing left to do but cajole and humour his granddaughter till both got home. Grandpa swore never again to step out of the house with me without a bottle of water and of Schweppes even when we were going a few houses down the road!

Then there was an evening ritual that we would go through with the regularity of clockwork. It began quite by accident. One day I happened to have left my teddy bear—very much a favourite though the stuffing had begun to spill out a little—on his bed. Grandfather in those days would turn in for the night every day at about 9 pm, come winter or summer, the only exception being when we had visitors. That particular evening Grandma was busy downstairs in the kitchen, I was in my room trying to write a few lines on an 'aerogramme' to parents who were in Delhi, when I heard some muttering that gradually grew louder and louder. I

Satarupa with her grandparents and mother, Oxford.

heard Grandpa shuffling about in his room. After a while, I went to investigate…he was in his *dhoti* and pullover outfit but without his glasses…he was continuing to mutter… 'Miserable bear'…'Miserable bear'. On seeing me he pointed to the 'miserable bear' and said he couldn't at all understand how the bear came to be in his room and on his bed. He seemed even more surprised to see me rolling about helplessly with laughter. Asking for the 'bear' to be banished from the room only served to turn this into a game and every evening Grandfather would discover various toys and dolls hidden away among the layers of sheets and blankets on his bed.

Grandfather, no matter how much he tried, could not avoid having the 'miserable bear' jump out at him from all sorts of unsuspecting places in the room. Every evening he would shake out his blankets and sheets before retiring to bed and peer around suspiciously to see if things that didn't belong to the room would suddenly emerge, all the while looking as surprised as the first evening when they did. He would mutter to himself, *'Eta Ki?'* ('What's this?') and then answer, 'It's those miserable creatures again.' This would carry on till each and every item had been fished out and tossed on to the floor. It soon became evident that I wasn't the only one enjoying the game!

As the years went by and one vacation with grandparents led to another, glimpses into 'timeless England' continued and so did the humour, the jokes and the pranks. One of the favourite anecdotes that NCC would relate was about 'posing'. It seems in the early 1920s he was on a train out of Calcutta and had three young men in a marginally inebriated and high-spirited state around him. The morning daily was being perused and one of the headlines that had something to do with Uday Shanker's 'poses that charmed Anna Pavlova' was being discussed by the young men. Grandpa was the onlooker. One of the young men asked in Bengali, '*Poses mane ki*?' ('What does 'poses' mean?'). Grandfather gleefully relating this episode to us, stood up and raised his arms in a wonderful mimicking action of the young man who replied. He said, '*Dakh aami kemon lengche lengche choli*.' (Young man dragging his left leg behind him in a semi-dance mode on a moving train!) Grandpa reproducing this for us perfectly! 'You 'poses' *me mane tui o sherkhom lengche lengche cholish*.' More play-acting would follow which in turn would raise howls of laughter from us. Grandpa enjoying this to the hilt, grinning and, winking mischieviously, would always oblige us with an encore!

There was some humour that was directed at Grandma as well. Having a great fetish for polishing things from leather to furniture, he had a vast array of waxes, polishes and sprays, several of which had strong odours and some even gave off slightly unpleasant fumes. Grandma, quite legitimately, given the breathing troubles she had developed in those years, frowned down upon the fervent bouts of polishing undertaken by Grandpa. Grandpa in concession to her would therefore begin the polishing only when Grandma had retired upstairs for her afternoon siesta. Doors downstairs would be opened; tables, shoes or even books would begin to be shined. I, of course, had to be a partner in such crimes, fetching this, putting that away, switching on the exhausts, etc, while Grandpa would whisper while winking at me, '*Uni ekdom pochchondo korben na…ekkebare gondho na jaye opore*.' ('She won't like it at all…none of the odours should reach her at all.') That was quite a tall order given the kind of house it was. A few minutes later the inevitable would happen. Grandma would call out from upstairs and I would have to rush up and face an inquisition about why Grandpa had started polishing again. It would usually be because we were expecting visitors or a new object had been bought and for its worthy maintenance such acts had to be regularly indulged in.

Once I was at the receiving end of the polishing. I had just bought a pair of lace-up shoes with tastefully stitched uppers from

Serving wine to his neighbour, Professor Thomas, while Satarupa, Emily and Anne Thomas look on.

a preferred store. Being very pleased with myself at having found this 'exactly-what-I-was-looking-for' pair, I made the mistake of showing it to Grandfather. He seemed to approve of it though he muttered something under his breath which I didn't quite catch. In the meanwhile I went upstairs to have a chat with Grandma and by the time I returned I couldn't believe my eyes. My shoes, which had been a lovely light tan, were now looking an indescribable colour, somewhere between grey and slush! It wasn't a happy moment for Grandpa or me, tears sprang to my eyes, Grandpa tried explaining that a certain kind of polish and a softener should be applied to new shoes before they are worn but in the absence of an exactly matching shade of polish, he had used what was available in the house. The upshot of this exchange was that he vanished from the house within a few minutes saying he was going to the nearby market. I did my best to stop him but there was no turning him back. The turpentine had to be fetched and the shoes had to be cleaned up. And so it was done. The shoes took a good two days to dry after the turpentine treatment, Grandpa and I peering at them every now and again and lo behold on the third day, once they had completely dried, they had returned not to the original light tan but to a dark tan…giving them, in retrospect, a better shade than the original!

If the news of impending visitors set off a bout of polishing, then the excitement about the comestibles to be offered was no less. This enthusiasm was equally shared by Grandpa and Grandma but the route to agreement was often marked by differences as to the exact nature of the menu. When it came to a visit from the family then the excitement ran possibly even higher. Such occasions were preceded by many shopping expeditions to the city centre undertaken with great gusto by Grandpa, accompanied by granddaughter if she happened to be in Oxford, collecting the best of Angel cakes or Eccles cakes, crumpets, Baba au Rhums (never being allowed to call them Rum Babas!), lobster bisques, packets of smoked salmon, kettle chips, pickled gherkins, etc. There would be visits to the delicatessen for the best in cheeses (the strongly flavoured blue stilton was a must) as well as the best in sausages and cold cuts. This was followed by a visit to the pâtisserie for croissants, pecan pies and various kinds of gateau. The shopping list nearly always tilted a little more towards the sweeter range of delectables, inevitably so because NCC had a great penchant for confections particularly the ones that went by the names of 'marzipan' and 'Turkish Delight'.

No matter how impressive the shopping list, Amiya Chaudhurani or Grandma was never content to serve only what had been fetched from the shops, she would spend hours painstakingly cooking, baking, garnishing and decorating. The result—there were more than a few who would drop in for a meal whenever the chance should present itself. Pot luck or by invitation, food and drink had to be given their due regard!

As many would be familiar, the spoken word was accorded an equally high place of honour by Grandfather, the more the number of visitors, the more he spoke. Grandmother would say, 'You know how much your Grandpa likes to talk...when we have visitors he goes on and on till he is ready to drop... and we at home are left to the task of helping him recuperate once the visitors have left.' It is perhaps superfluous to mention here that most of the visitors usually were ready to drop much before he was! When confronted with Grandma's comments, his classic reply with a chuckle would be: 'You know your Grandmother has coined this term for all my talk but after all I once made a living out of talking!'

Current thoughts, writings, favourite books and authors, paintings, objets d'art and their lighting, wines, hats, shoes, attire were all discussed at great length but what often took the centre stage was music. NCC's interest in Western classical music has perhaps been often talked about but his keen ear and consequent obsession with perfecting his high-fidelity equipment not so much. From the purchase of the equipment to the correct placing of the speakers vis-à-vis the amplifier and the record player—nothing was left to chance. He was extremely particular about where the listener was supposed to sit, be it to listen to an operatic aria or to the Tagore song lately haunting him. Nothing could be treated casually. All the acoustically relevant distances would be measured and fixed by means of a rope that he kept handy; various

Nirad Chaudhuri used to discuss his favourite books and authors with Satarupa.

improvements had to be made including the use of ballasts to tilt the huge speakers at a particular angle, the use of felt mats on the turntable and the fixing of its pods using rather unusual mediums. I had to be the patient listener in more senses than one. Every time an adjustment was made, even of a millimetre, I had to listen to and comment on the minutest differences that had come into play after various test-records and other relevant pieces of music had been played at different volumes. The forum for discussing the nuances of the composition was distinct from this exercise. During these sessions one was not supposed to get carried away by the music! This exercise, to which I was no stranger having begun young as a commentator for my Dad's hi-fi system, was not without its benefits. It certainly helped in developing a keen ear and I have to acknowledge that it was thrilling to be appreciated for one's comments.

The partnership regarding the hi-fi system went further. On one of our trips into town, I had been introduced to this rather pleasant and courteous young man at the store that Grandpa frequented for his hi-fidelity equipment. It was, predictably enough, a store that specialised in providing customised equipment for the more discerning listeners. When Grandpa started finding 'popping' into town every now and again a little difficult, I would be regularly dispatched to the store to fetch the 'necessary' items beginning with cleaning fluids and brushes for LPs, several kinds of cables, and finally to buy needles for his cartridges. It was a chore I didn't dislike, sometimes spending quite a while in the store discussing what made moving coil cartridges so special, or the differences in sound quality between LPs and cassettes, and later between LPs and CDs, which had just about begun to come in. The hi-fi and tinkering bug had affected quite a few in the family to the extent that we would never again be comfortable listening to anything that sounded remotely tinny or would always be driven to dismantle equipment beginning with record players, cassette recorders and walkmans!

From the world of books and literature so much was discussed that it would be difficult to render it here in true spirit. But suffice it to say that we shared a fascination for Austen, that I was introduced to a mesmerising world of François-René de Chateaubriand, Honoré de Balzac, Anatole France, La Rochefoucauld and others; Grandpa sometimes reading aloud in chaste French. On one of the trips to Oxford while still in school, I was directed to read Henry James's *The Portrait of a Lady* without further ado. There were of course many books in his library that I would devour without being told, amongst them a fantastic collection of Sherlock Holmes.

Just as we hugely agreed over Jane Austen, Charlotte Bronte and Henry James, we sometimes disagreed over politics and the presence of the neighbour's cat, whom I adored, in our garden. I realised that trying to radically change his opinion in one shot was futile but observed that with time he himself would mellow on various issues, the cat being the easiest. Dogs he loved and stopped to admire whenever possible but Flossie's presence in the garden he didn't much care for, having found her digging in the region of carefully planted crocus bulbs one morning.

The 20 Lathbury Road house and garden had so many memories and associations that it was no coincidence that when the Oxfordshire Blue Plaques Board decided to put up a blue plaque in honour of NCC, it was to be placed on the gatepost right outside this house he had lived in for seventeen years. It would be thanks to Sir Hugo Brunner, Lord Lieutenant of Oxford from 1996 to 2008 and the founder of the Oxfordshire Blue Plaques scheme, that this wonderful and rare event would come to pass.

Above: Unveiling of the plaque by author Amit Chaudhuri, Satarupa and Vikram (Nirad Chaudhuri's grandson), October 2008. Photograph courtesy Moira Pavelin. Right: Blue plaque at 20 Lathbury Road. Photograph by Satarupa Chaudhuri.

On 4 October 2008, during the course of a rather wind-blown afternoon, the velvet curtain covering the sparkling blue plaque was drawn away by Amit Chaudhuri, my cousin Vik and me while Sir Hugo and many friends as well as well-wishers cheered, amongst them the honourable dignitaries of the Indian High Commission in London. Sir Hugo Brunner spoke warmly and eloquently of his long association with NCC, one that had begun when he was Grandfather's publisher at Chatto and Windus, and one that had endured very well over the years. Amit Chaudhuri very much in the spirit of the afternoon spoke candidly amongst other things of his fleeting meeting with NCC and his apprehensions about being grilled by the man should he have decided to visit 20 Lathbury Road!

The blue plaque ceremony was then followed by a lovely tea-party for all the guests at Hugo and Mary Rose's house on Norham Road in Oxford. For my cousin Vik and me, it was an occasion to remember, courtesy a grandfather who had passed away nine years earlier but who would be remembered thanks to the blue plaque for many more years to come.

Satarupa Chaudhuri

A Requiem for

Nirad C. Chaudhuri

The last photograph of Nirad Chaudhuri taken by Dhruva.

Nirad C. Chaudhuri, Hon. Commander of British Empire, Hon. D. Lit (Oxford), Hon. Doctorate, University of Stirling, Scotland, Fellow of the Royal Literary Society, London, died on 1 August, 1999, at the age of one hundred-and-one years, eight months and eight days. It was just twenty-one weeks short of touching the new millennium. For the last five years of his life, Father, the 'Unknown Indian', would often write and talk about death as the inevitable destiny for every living being and, as no one knew when that would happen, he seemed to have reconciled with the fact that his days were coming to an end.

My illustrious father, who was no longer an 'Unknown Indian', retained his Indian nationality as well as his Indian passport till the last moment

Nirad Chaudhuri's footprints in the snow, outside 20 Lathbury Road.

of his life. When mourners coming from several countries of the world paid respect by showering rose petals on his mortal remains at the crematorium in Oxford, they might have been agreeably surprised to see Nirad Chaudhuri, the proverbial last Englishman of the twentieth century, as per his last wishes, dressed in a fine silk *dhoti* and a *kurta* like a true Bengali *bhadralok* (gentleman). Thus, even in death, Father had proved his oft-repeated saying that he was proud to be a Bengali first, then a Hindu, and last, but not the least, an Indian!

Dhruva N. Chaudhuri

Index

D

E

F

G

H

I

J

K

S

T

U

V

W